PICK YOUR BRAINS
about

USA

Jane Egginton

Illustrations by
Caspar Williams & Craig Dixon

CADOGAN

C408774357

Acknowledgements
The author and the publisher would like to thank 'guest editor'
James C. White (aged 13).

Special thanks to Hollie O'Connor

Published by Cadogan Guides 2005
Copyright © Jane Egginton 2005

The moral right of Jane Egginton to be identified as the author of this work has been
asserted by her in accordance with the Copyright, Designs and Patents Act 1988.

All rights reserved. No part of this publication may be reproduced, stored in a
retrieval system, or transmitted, in any form or by any means, electronic or
mechanical, including photocopying and recording, or by any information
storage and retrieval system except as may be expressly permitted
by the UK 1988 Copyright Design & Patents Act and the USA 1976 Copyright
Act or in writing from the publisher. Requests for permission should be
addressed to Cadogan Guides, Network House, 1 Ariel Way, London W12 7SL in
the UK; or The Globe Pequot Press, PO Box 480, Guilford, Connecticut
06437–0480, in the USA.

Illustrations by Caspar Williams and Craig Dixon
Illustrations and map copyright © Cadogan Guides 2005
Map by ⓉⓌ

Cadogan Guides
Network House, 1 Ariel Way, London W12 7SL
info@cadoganguides.co.uk
www.cadoganguides.com

The Globe Pequot Press
246 Goose Lane, PO Box 480, Guilford,
Connecticut 06437–0480

Design and typesetting by Mathew Lyons
Printed in Italy by Legoprint

A catalogue record for this book is available
from the British Library
ISBN 1-86011-222-6

SOUTH LANARKSHIRE LIBRARIES

Contents

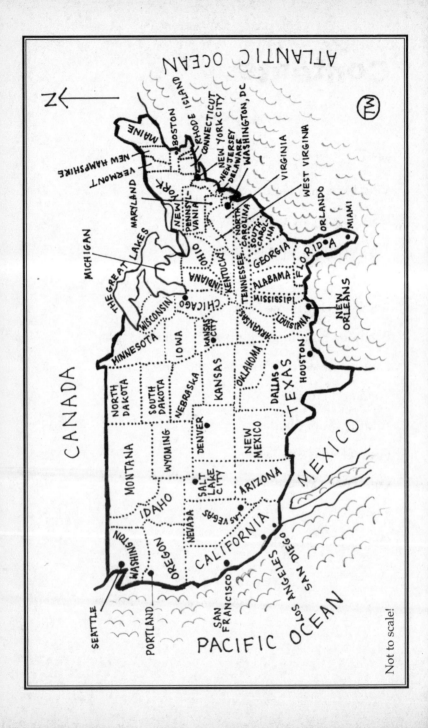

Vital Facts
and Figures

Name: The word 'America' comes from the name of an Italian, Amerigo Vespucci (1454–1512), one of the first European explorers of the 'New World' (North, Central and South America). Vespucci never visited what is now the USA, yet the people who live there call themselves Americans. Their country's full name is the United States of America, but it is called the United States, the USA, the US or just the States for short.

Population and area: There are 293 million people living in the USA. It's the world's third-largest country (after Russia and Canada), and covers about 3,618,000 square miles (about 9,370,000 square kilometres). It is around half the size of Russia, slightly larger than China, about two and a half times the size of western Europe and 70 times the size of England!

If you were to take a taxi from New York City, on the east coast of the USA, to Los Angeles, on the west coast, it would cost you around £3,500!

It is 3,460 miles (about 5,568 kilometres) from New York to London and 3,620 miles (about 5,825 kilometres) from New York to Paris.

Americans are usually described as being one of five groups: White (also called Caucasian); African-American (also called Black); Hispanic, (also called Latino – around one in seven of people living in the USA are Hispanics, who come from Mexico and South and Central America.); Asian American; and Native American (also called American

Indian). Many Americans are related to the immigrants who first came over from Europe – especially from Germany, Ireland, Scotland, England, Italy and Poland.

Borders and coasts: The USA shares the continent of North America with two other countries, Canada to the north and Mexico to the south. These three countries have some of the longest borders in the world.

The main part of the USA has coasts on the Pacific Ocean, the Atlantic Ocean and the Caribbean Sea, but two of its 50 states are separated from this part: Alaska, which is far to the north, is separated from the rest of the USA by Canada and has coasts on the Bering Sea and the Arctic Ocean; and Hawaii, which is a group of islands in the Pacific.

Geography: There are hills and low mountains all along the eastern coast of the USA, which is made up of three regions: New England, the Mid-Atlantic states and the South. The

mountains
include the Appalachians, which
run parallel to the east coast from Canada all the way south
to the state of Alabama.

To the west of the Appalachians is an enormous plain in
the centre, or the Midwest, a region that includes the prairies
or Great Plains. West of these are the Southwestern states,
forming a region of deserts and high plateaus, and then the
Rocky Mountains.

Between the Rockies and the Sierra Nevada mountains of
California lies more desert.

Alaska has wide river valleys and Hawaii has lots of
volcanoes. Nevada is the driest state.

The lowest point in the USA is Death Valley, which lies
about 280 feet (86 metres) below sea level. The highest point
is Mount McKinley in Alaska, at 20,320 feet (6,194 metres).

Rivers: The D river in the state of Oregon is not only the
shortest river in the country, but the shortest in the world!
It's only 120 feet (37 metres) long. Although the Missouri

River is 2,466 miles (3,968 kilometres) long and the Mississippi River is 2,348 miles (3,779 kilometres) long, the Mississippi is known as the longest river in the USA because it is continuous.

Lakes: The Great Lakes are a group of five large lakes on or near the border between the United States and Canada. They are the largest group of fresh-water lakes on the Earth, and the Great Lakes–St Lawrence River system is the largest fresh-water system in the world. The Great Lakes are sometimes referred to as inland seas.

The Great Lakes are:

- ☞ Lake Superior (the largest and deepest)
- ☞ Lake Michigan (the only one entirely in the US and the second-largest by volume)
- ☞ Lake Huron (the second-largest by area)
- ☞ Lake Erie (the smallest by volume and the shallowest)
- ☞ Lake Ontario (the smallest in area, and on much lower ground than the rest).

A commonly used way of remembering the names of the lakes is 'HOMES', for 'Huron, Ontario, Michigan, Erie, Superior'.

Weather: The USA is such a large country that there is often sunshine in one part of the country while it is snowing in another. Places like Hawaii and Florida in the south are tropical and often hot. Alaska in the north usually has snow, ice and bitter winters.

The USA also has some of the most dramatic weather in the world. In a normal year it has around 10,000 really big thunderstorms, 5,000 floods, 1,000 tornados and several hurricanes!

On the road: Route 66 is still one of the most famous roads in the world, even though many sections of it have been

replaced by highways/freeways (which are like motorways). Work began in 1925 on Route 66, which joined Chicago to Los Angeles, 2,448 miles (3,940 kilometres) away. It crossed eight states and three different time zones! The road has been written about in a television programme, and in books and songs – the most famous song, by Bobby Troup, talks about the excitement of making the trip to California and getting kicks on Route 66!

The USA is a really enormous country. In some places, if someone tells you that something is just around the corner, they could mean that it's half a day's drive away.

In most towns and cities, roads are straight and form a grid made up of squares. This makes it very hard to get lost.

Americans drive on the right. They love their cars, and the bigger and faster they are, the better. Most Americans hate to walk. Some places in the USA can only be reached if you have a car. After all, the drive-in cinema and the drive-in McDonald's were invented here, so that if you want to watch a film or eat you don't even have to get out of your car!

Speed limits are different depending on what state you are in, but are normally 65 mph, 70 mph or 75 mph on interstate highways/freeways. (Very few Americans know the metric system, so distances are all still in miles.)

Time zones: The continental USA has four time zones:

☞ Eastern Time (GMT (Greenwich Mean Time) minus five hours) in New England, the Mid-Atlantic states and the South

☞ Central Time (GMT minus six hours) in most of the Midwest and parts of the Southwest

☞ Mountain Time (GMT minus seven hours) in the Rockies and other parts of the Midwest and the Southwest

☞ Pacific Time (GMT minus eight hours) on the west coast (California, Oregon and Washington states)

Alaska and Hawaii cover two more time zones. Alaska Time is GMT minus nine hours and Hawaii–Aleutian Time is GMT minus 10 hours. (The Aleutians are a string of islands to the west of Alaska.)

Did you know that the United States did not need time zones until long-distance trains arrived? Then for the first time it was possible to travel hundreds of miles in one day.

Trains, planes, automobiles and…greyhounds: Trains are not as popular in the USA as they are in a lot of other countries as internal flights are usually a much quicker way of travelling long distance across the country. But trains are common for travelling shorter distances from main cities into the country or commuting to work. Buses are often used for town and city travel but in country areas this may be difficult. The Greyhound Bus line is popular for long-distance travel as it is good value and it covers a lot of the country. Many Americans use their cars to get around for short and long distances. In certain cities such as Los

Angeles, practically everybody has a car as local transport is not very good.

Airports: There are nearly 6,000 airports in the USA, more than in any other country in the world. In the next ten years more than 1 billion people a year will get on planes in the United States!

You have to be careful when flying or even driving from one part of the USA to another because you may cross one or more time zones. This means you must sometimes change your watch when in the air if going from one side of the country to the other! It is not unknown for people to miss their flights because they think they are in another time zone.

It takes a long time to fly from one side of the USA to another. It is a five-hour flight from San Francisco in the west to New York in the east – longer than it takes to fly from England to Morocco in Africa!

Major cities: The capital city is Washington, DC (population 572,000). Other major cities are:

☞ New York City, in New York State (8,039,000)

☞ Los Angeles, in California (3,829,000)

☞ Chicago, in Illinois (2,926,000)

☞ Houston, in Texas (2,043,000)

☞ Philadelphia, in Pennsylvania (1,519,000)

☞ Phoenix, in Arizona (1,410,000)

☞ San Diego, in California (1,269,000)

☞ Dallas, in Texas (1,243,000).

Independence: The United States declared independence from Great Britain on 4 July 1776. At that time it had just 13 states, all on the east coast. The other 37 states joined over the following years.

Flag: The American flag has 13 stripes of red and white running horizontally, standing for the 13 British colonies that became the original United States. A blue rectangle in the corner has 50 small white stars in rows. These stars represent the 50 states.

The President: The President of the United States is the head of state of the country. He is also the chief executive of the federal (central) government and commander-in-chief of the armed forces. The current President of the United States is George W. Bush. Because the United States is so powerful, the country is sometimes known as a 'Superpower'.

The early rulers of the USA were known as the Founding Fathers. They wanted to create a government that did not allow one person to have too much control in the way that the British monarchy had at that time. So they wrote a document known as the Constitution that outlined a system of government and rule, which ensured that the 'powers'

The United States has some very funny place names too:

☞ Nutsville is a town in West Virginia

☞ Normal is in Illinois

☞ Ding Dong is a place in Texas

☞ Monkey's Eyebrow is a real town in the state of Arizona

☞ People really live in Two Egg in Florida.

WELCOME TO
TWO EGG
FLORIDA

☞ Then there is Hell in Michigan. The story goes that when they were deciding on a name, someone shouted: 'You all can go to Hell, and you can call this place Hell for all I care.'

☞ Perhaps a more pleasant place to live would be Tranquillity, in northern California. It's got to be better than coming from Gas in Kansas or Tightwad in Missouri, even though the people there insist they are not mean!

☞ Dull in Ohio is certainly not boring, because Boring is a place in Oregon, while Nothing is in Arizona.

☞ There is a history behind some names: Sweetlips in Tennessee is where soldiers in the Civil War stopped to get water. You can probably guess how Fleatown in Ohio got named.

16

were separated. They are known as the legislative, executive, and judicial powers.

Each of these three branches of the US Government has its own responsibilities but they also work together to run the country.

The state of each state: Each of the states in the US has its own Governor voted for by the people who live there. This means that different states have their own laws, some of which reflect things that are of local interest to that state and have evolved over many years. All states, however, also answer to federal laws, so there is a sharing of power between the central government and the individual states.

Languages: People have come from every other country in the world to live in the US, bringing their languages and customs with them, and many Native Americans still use their own languages too. But among all the hundreds of languages spoken in the USA, English is the one that is used for the law and understood throughout the country; however, Spanish is the second most common language (spoken by about 28.1 million people). Creole and Cajun, a kind of French, are spoken in some parts of Louisiana.

Three states are officially bilingual: Hawaii (English and Hawaiian), Louisiana (English and French) and New Mexico (English and Spanish).

Some place names: Many places in the United States, especially on the east coast, have names that were brought from Britain or Ireland, either unchanged (such as Boston in Massachusetts, Albany in New York State, the 17 different Dublins), or with 'New' put in front of them (such as New York, New Hampshire, New Jersey). Many other place names come from Native American languages (such as the states of Massachusetts, Tennessee or Ohio, or the city of Chicago). Others again come from Spanish (such as San Diego, Los Angeles or Florida).

Monetary unit: The US currency is the dollar, which is divided into 100 cents. Dollars are often called 'greenbacks' because all the banknotes (which Americans call bills) have designs in black, white and green.

The Internet domain: us

Films and television: More films are made in the US than in any other country in the world. Film-making started in New York State, but for nearly 100 years the industry has been centred on Hollywood in California, where the weather is usually fine, the light is great for filming and land for studios used to be very cheap.

One hundred and fifty homes in New York City got the first televisions in the country in 1936. The first programme was a cartoon from the series *Felix the Cat*. Since then television has expanded to hundreds of stations, on cable and satellite, and US programmes are watched all over the world.

USA
History in
a Nutshell

In the beginning...

No-one knows exactly when the men and women who would become known as Native Americans – also known as American Indians – first walked on the American continent. The best guesses are sometime between 10,000 and 30,000 years ago. What most experts do agree, however, is that the first Native Americans came here on foot across what is now the Bering Strait between Alaska and Siberia, walking along a 'land bridge' between the two continents that has since sunk beneath the sea.

The Americas – as the continents of North and South America are sometimes known – were 'discovered' by Christopher Columbus in 1492. But he probably wasn't the first. Some people believe that the Chinese discovered them in 1421. Others believe that a Welsh explorer called Prince Madoc landed in Mobile Bay in the Gulf of Mexico in 1170. Another belief is that Vikings arrived first – around the year 1000. Then there is the legend of St Brendan, the Irish Christian missionary, who, it is said, landed in Newfoundland in the sixth century.

The European settlers

In the two centuries after Columbus's discovery, the leading European nations established colonies in North America. The French held a vast but largely unpopulated territory right down from what is now Canada through the Mid West and down to New Orleans. They called it New France. The Dutch, meanwhile, held what is now New York City (except they called it New Amsterdam!). And the Swedes had what they called – guess what? – New Sweden, which was roughly where Delaware is today. (New England, of course, still exists, as does *Nova Scotia* – Latin for New Scotland!)

The Trail of Tears

The early settlers relied heavily on the help of the Native Americans. But as the European populations expanded, they took over the Native American's ancient homelands – often by force – and evicted them. Over the next two hundred years the Native Americans would be driven west and their way of life destroyed.

The Native Americans weren't the only victims. The bison or buffalo is the largest land mammal in North America. When Columbus arrived there were as many as 100 million roaming the Great Plains. But by the end of the 19th century there were as few as 750 left. They had been hunted in such

You can see Native America in...

☞ **Crazy Horse Memorial** Carved out of the living rock face in South Dakota, at 600 feet tall, this will eventually be the world's largest sculpture. Work began in 1948. When finished it will show Crazy Horse on horseback pointing to the horizon. The inscription will be: 'My lands are where my dead lie buried'.

☞ **The 'Trail of Tears' National Historic Trail** You can trace the route along which the Cherokee Indians were forced to move from Georgia to Oklahoma in 1838. The name is that given to the tragic event by the Cherokees themselves.

huge numbers to stop the great herds interfering with the railways that were being laid across the continent. Thankfully, there are now around 350,000 of these great animals left.

The first Thanksgiving

Probably the most famous early colony was that of Plymouth, Massachusetts, founded in 1620 by a group now known as the Pilgrim Fathers, who were in fact Puritans fleeing from religious persecution in their native England. They came across the Atlantic on a ship called the *Mayflower*, intending to settle in the area around what is now New York. However, they got blown off course and landed instead near Cape Cod on 11 November. Deciding not to go any further, they stayed put, naming their new home after the English port they had left 65 days earlier.

Because they arrived with little time to spare before the winter set in, the settlers experienced great hardship in their first year. When, the following autumn, their harvest was good, they celebrated with a three-day feast.

Over the next few decades, it became traditional to feast

at the end of bountiful harvests. But it wasn't until 1863 that the Thanksgiving holiday became a fixed annual, nationwide event.

Many of the colonies failed to prosper, but the planting of tobacco, in particular, brought increasing wealth. However, the need for cheap labour to work in the fields also brought the slave trade. All the European Empires and colonies on the American continents were supported by slavery: in the 18th century alone six million men, women and children were transported by ship from the West Coast of Africa in terrible conditions.

You can see colonial America in...

☞ **Spanish missions** Between 1769 and 1823, Spanish missionaries built 21 missions along the California coast between San Diego and San Francisco to convert the Native Americans to Christianity. They are strung along a road that the Spanish knew as *El Camino Real*, the King's Highway, but which is known today as Highway 101.

☞ **Pilgrim Fathers** Just outside Plymouth, Massachussetts is Plimoth Plantation, a living recreation of an English settlement in 1627.

Taxing problems

The European powers fought endlessly to control the American colonies. Ultimately, however, the British won control. The government in London started to impose taxes on their American colonies. But the colonies resented having to pay high taxes to a government so far away and which didn't represent them.

The Boston Tea Party

One of the most controversial taxes was on the import of tea! In 1773, the British government allowed the East India Company to sell tea to the American colonies without having to pay the tax that the American traders had to pay. The colonies were outraged. At many ports, East India Company ships weren't even allowed to land. They did, however, manage to get into the harbour at Boston and planned to put the tea ashore – by force if necessary.

Locals got wind of this and on the night of 16 December 1773, a 60-strong group of Bostonians calling themselves the Sons of Liberty dressed themselves as Mohawks and boarded the three East India Company ships in the harbour. Although they smashed all the cases of tea and threw their contents into the sea, they seem to have been remarkably polite otherwise. It is said that they took off their shoes and even swept the decks afterwards!

Strange as it may seem, this disagreement over tax nearly 250 years ago is the main reason why a lot of Americans stopped drinking tea and started drinking coffee instead.

The War of Independence

It wasn't long before the colonies were at all-out war with the British. The opening shots actually occurred on the night of 18th April 1775, when the British army – based in Boston – moved under cover of darkness to take control of the weapons of the American soldiers at Concord, Massachussetts. But an American called Paul Revere rode out ahead of the British, raising the alarm and alerting the people of Concord and Lexington that the army was heading their way. Legend has it that despite instructions to be as quiet as possible, Revere shouted out warnings as he rode along! Thinking they had surprise on their side, the British had only sent out 700 men. But, thanks to Revere, they now faced several thousand American soldiers. The British fled back to Boston and the war had begun.

The pursuit of happiness

It would be five years before the British would finally admit defeat (and a further two before it was officially marked in the Treaty of Paris of 1783 in which the two countries agreed to peace). But the Americans were well ahead of them. They had produced their Declaration of Independence on 4 July 1776. It is one of the most inspirational documents ever written, containing as it does the then revolutionary idea that all men are created equal and have a natural-born right to 'life, liberty and the pursuit of happiness'. Equally important would be the Bill of Rights attached to the Constitution when it came to be drafted 11 years later, which promises the right of American people to freedom of speech, freedom of worship and freedom of the press. These were very radical ideas for the time.

It's hard to imagine, but actually, the USA when it first came into being, only contained 13 states running down the eastern coast. They roughly compare to the following states today: North Carolina, South Carolina, Connecticut, Delaware, Georgia, Kentucky, Maine, Maryland, Massachusetts, New Hampshire, New Jersey, New York, Pennsylvania, Rhode Island, Tennessee, Vermont, and Virginia.

You can see independent America in...

☞ **Paul Revere's house** The oldest building in Boston – and the one from which Revere made his famous ride

☞ **Valley Forge** The camp in Pennsylvania where George Washington created the army that would defeat Britain's professional soldiers from tens of thousands of ordinary men and women

The Louisiana Purchase

Most of Texas and California were Mexican until 1846. The biggest expansion of the United States occurred in 1803 when America doubled in size overnight in what is known as the Lousiana Purchase. For just $13 million, the US government bought not just present day Louisiana, but some or all of these states too: Arkansas, Colorado, North Dakota, South Dakota, Iowa, Kansas, Minnesota, Missouri, Montana, New Mexico, Oklahoma, Texas and Wyoming – in fact, more than a quarter of today's country. The funny thing is that the US government had only wanted to buy New Orleans! The then president, Thomas Jefferson was astonished when the French offered the sale of over 800,000 extra square miles at approximately two cents an acre.

But the French refused to tell the Americans where the

western border was so they simply didn't know what land they had bought. So the US government funded an expedition – known as the Corps of Discovery – to explore the new territories all the way to the Pacific Ocean. Jefferson hoped there would be a river crossing the continent for transporting goods across the country.

Lewis and Clark

The Corps of Discovery set off up the Missouri River on 14 May 1804. Before they reached journey's end on 7 November 1805 at the place where the Columbia River meets the Pacific Ocean, they would travel nearly 4,000 miles on foot or horseback, or by boat.

The first 2,000 miles were spent rowing upriver; when the current was too strong to row against, they towed their boats along the river bank. When they gave up on the Missouri and headed west for the sea, they had to climb the Rocky Mountains in bitter cold, close to starvation. Along they way, they were joined by a French fur-trapper, Toussaint Charbonneau, and his Shoshone Indian wife, Sacagawea. She was only 16 years old. The couple, who had been living with the Hidatsa Indians, joined Lewis and Clark as interpreters. Sacagawea would talk with her fellow Native Americans and translate from Shoshone to Hidatsa as the two tribes spoke different languages. Charbonneau would translate Hidatsa into French, and then one or two other members of the team would translate that into English.

Because war parties wouldn't take women, Sacagawea was seen as a sign of peace by the Indian tribes and is today recognised as a symbol of American women. Sacagawea also gave birth to a boy, Jean-Baptiste, and then carried him all the way to the Pacific and back. She is commemorated today on one side of the US dollar coin, pictured carrying her young son in a papoose (a kind of sling Native Americans used to carry babies) on her back.

Jefferson was wrong about there being a river across the continent. But then, he was wrong about a lot of other things too: he thought Lewis and Clark would also encounter woolly mammoths and a mountain made of salt. But what Lewis and Clark did find – together with the epic success of their journey – made them national heroes.

Civil war

But it wouldn't be the east and west that would divide the United States in the 19th century; it would be the north and south. The two regions were entirely different: the wealth of the largely rural south was based on crops like cotton, for which slave labour was used; the 'free' north was increasingly industrial and urban. The north had abolished slavery at the turn of the century and ever since had been attempting to ban it nationwide.

By 1860, the southern states had had enough of what they saw as people in the north interfering. The election of President Abraham Lincoln, a leader in the movement to end slavery, was the last straw. Seven states in the south separated from the Union (the rest of the United States) to form the Confederate States of America. They were soon joined by another four states. With the north unwilling to either accept the break-up of the nation or to see slavery remain, war broke out.

The American civil war was a terrible conflict which literally divided families against each other. More than a million Americans lost their lives before the war ended in 1865 with the surrender of the south. The north had been so confident of victory that it initially only asked for volunteers for the army for 90 days. However, it was the Confederacy (the seven states in the south) that dominated the first two years of fighting, under its legendary general, Robert E. Lee. The turning point came over three baking hot days in July 1863 when the northern army defeated Lee's forces at the Battle of Gettysburg in Pennsylvania.

You can see Civil War America in...

☞ **Fort Sumter** This island in the harbour at Charleston, South Carolina was where the first shots of the Civil War were fired on 12 April 1861

☞ **Gettysburg** The Gettysburg National Military Park in Pennsylvania marks the site of this pivotal battle in the Civil War, in which some 50,000 men were killed or wounded.

Pioneer trails

In 1862 President Lincoln signed one of the most significant laws in American history: the Homestead Act. This gave people the right to claim 160 acres of land in one of 30 states – which basically meant all those that had been added to the country since the Declaration of Independence. If you lived on a plot of land for five years, farmed it and built a house you could buy it.

Excited by this opportunity, men and women flooded westward, enduring great hardships as the only means of transport were in wagons, on horseback or on foot.

It was this pioneering period that saw some of the most violent conflicts between the European immigrants and the Native Americans, whose ancestral lands were being taken from them by the settlers. Most such battles resulted in widescale destruction for the Native Americans. The most famous exception to this is the Battle of Little Bighorn in Montana in June 1876 when Sitting Bull and Crazy Horse led their Native American warriors from the Sioux and Cheyenne tribes against a US cavalry unit led by Lieutenant Colonel Custer. Also known as Custer's Last Stand, the battle saw the entire US unit destroyed.

You can see pioneer America in...

☞ **Coloma Valley** The Marshall Gold Discovery State Historic Park marks the site of James Marshall's discovery of Californian gold. There is a working replica of Sutter's Mill and you can learn to 'pan', or search, for gold yourself, too!

☞ **Little Bighorn** Last Stand Hill in Montana, as it is known, has memorials to the people killed on both sides of the famous battle between the Sioux and Cheyenne Indians, led by Sitting Bull and Crazy Horse, and Colonel Custer's US cavalry.

Gold rush

It wasn't just the promise of free land that drew people westward. They also came because of the promise of gold!

The biggest gold rush – in California – began quietly enough on the morning of 24 January 1848, when James Marshall, who was building a sawmill for a rich man called John Sutter, saw something glinting in a nearby stream. He fished it out and showed it to Sutter. They both agreed it was gold and swore to keep it a secret. However, news got out and the story made a San Francisco newspaper on 15 March.

It has been estimated that some half-a-million people swarmed to California from around the world in search of their fortune. One lucky man found a 195 lb (88.5 kg) lump

of gold in 1854! But most faced poverty and starvation and by 1864, most of California's significant gold deposits were gone.

The American century

The 20th century has often been called the American century. The USA's industrial, economic and military strength mean that is has come to be at the centre of world affairs in the last 100 years. In 1903, Wilbur and Orville Wright made the first-ever flight in a powered aircraft at Kitty Hawk, North Carolina. Also in 1903, Henry Ford started the Ford Motor Company, producing the first mass-produced car, the Model-T Ford. By 1918, half of the cars in America were Model-Ts. In 1969, it became the first (and at that time only) country to put a man on the moon. America has seized the world's imagination and changed everyday life for everyone, everywhere.

☞ **The King Center** Dedicated to the life and work of Martin Luther King, this site in Atlanta, Georgia, includes the house he was born in.

☞ **Sun Studios** The birthplace of rock'n'roll in Memphis, Tennessee and the studios where Elvis Presley first recorded his music that would change the world!

☞ **National Air and Space Museum, Washington** It's all here – from the Wright Brothers' first aircraft to a command module from one of the Apollo space missions. (And if you've ever wanted to hold a bit of the moon in your hand, this is definitely the place for you!)

Needless to say, it has not always been peaceful. The USA has been part of many wars, particularly in the Second World War when it fought against Hitler and Nazi Germany, and it also played a major role in the Cold War between the democratic West and the

communist Soviet Union.

The Civil Rights Movement saw all Americans at last win the rights that had been promised to them in the Declaration of Independence and the Constitution. In the southern states, in particular, the abolition of slavery had done little to improve life for African-Americans. They were still treated like second-class citizens and segregation still existed so that they had to go to different  schools, use different toilets and enter buildings by different doors.

There were many small acts of great personal courage. One famous example is that of a woman called Rosa Parks who lived in Montgomery, Alabama. She was sitting at the back of the bus – which was where African-Americans had to sit by law – on her way home from work. Because the white section of the bus at the front was full, a white man came back and told her to give up her seat for him. She refused. For this she was arrested and thrown in prison.

As a result, a local minister called Martin Luther King led a year-long boycott of the bus service. He too was arrested. But eventually their case made its way to the Supreme Court, which ruled in Parks' favour. King would later become a world-famous figure in the civil rights movement and in 1964 won the Nobel Prize for his work. The same year would see the Civil Rights Act begin to redress many such wrongs.

Despite these problems, there's no doubt that America leads the world in many things. From Hollywood and the huge film and television industry, to music from blues, jazz to hip-hop, from Elvis Presley to iPods, from Microsoft to sport.

The American Dream

The United States of America is a young country – it's really only 200 or so years old. In that time millions of people from other countries around the globe have gone to live there. In fact, never in the history of the world has a country had so many people arriving with different languages, histories, and cultures.

Between 1892 and 1954 more than 17 million immigrants passed through Ellis Island, near New York City, on their way to becoming part of America's 'melting pot'. These people had a lot of hope for the country. This became known as the 'American Dream' and the USA became known as the 'land of opportunity'. The dream was not just about money

Did you know…

☞ There are more than 200 million telephones in the USA and lots of families have several telephone extensions around their homes, partly so that they can surf the Internet. Local telephone calls are free in the USA.

☞ Most homes, 98% in fact, have more than one television and many shows are shown over the entire country. There are 777 UHF commercial television stations, 589 VHF commercial television stations and several hundred educational stations.

and big houses and cars, although these have played a big part in it. It was also a hope that people would be recognised for who they were, not because of how important or rich their family is.

Bigger, faster

Fast food, fast cars, tall buildings, big portions… Things in the United States tend to be bigger and faster. The economy is now the largest on the planet (although, of course, that does not mean that every American is rich). The United States has only 5 per cent of the world's population, but it produces around 20 per cent of the world's coal, copper and petroleum. It produces nearly half of the world's corn and around one fifth of its beef, pork and lamb.

The United States is an enormous country, but there are still many wild parts. Even on the northeastern coast, where lots of people live, there are enormous empty spaces. In the Midwest there are states such as Wyoming, which is about the same size as France but has fewer than 500,000 people and thousands of wild animals.

Most people in the USA live in large cities. About 100 years ago more Americans lived in the countryside than in cities, because there was so much farming. In the past few

years, though, two
million more
Americans have
moved from large
cities to smaller
country towns
than the other way
around. Because the
USA is such a big
country and so many
people from different places came to live there, it has lots of
different customs, depending on which part of the country
you are in.

American symbols

Most people know about the American flag with its red and
white stripes from side to side. It is thought that a woman
called Betsy Ross was the first person to sew it. But not
everyone knows that there is another non-military flag,
which is meant to be used in peacetime. This one has stripes
from top to bottom, with blue stars on a white background.
The US Coast Guard and Customs use this kind of flag, but
they have their own symbol in place of the 50 stars.

On 8 July 1776 the Liberty Bell rang out in Philadelphia
(which was then the capital city) to tell people that the
Declaration of Independence was going to be read. Liberty
means freedom and the bell was first made in 1751 to
remember an agreement to protect the freedom of people all
over the world – this agreement of 1701 was called William
Penn's Charter of Privileges. Most Americans wanted to be
independent from Great Britain and particularly from the
British king at the time, George III.

The words of 'The Star-Spangled Banner', which is now
the US national anthem, were written by an American, but
the music is English! When Francis Scott Key saw American

soldiers beat the British at the Battle of Baltimore and the American flag flying over Fort McHenry in 1814, he changed the words of the song and called it 'The Star-Spangled Banner'. It was made the national anthem more than 100 years later, in 1931.

Before that the song that many Americans thought of as a kind of national anthem was 'Yankee Doodle Dandy'. It was sung during the French and Indian Wars by the British soldiers, who were making fun of the Americans. In the song 'Doodle' means 'fool'. Later, though, the Americans sang it for themselves during the American Revolution.

Uncle Sam

Uncle Sam is a tall old man with white hair and a white beard who usually dresses in the colours of the American flag – red, white and blue – and wears a top hat. His initials are the same as those of the United States and he is used as a symbol of the country.

Who was Uncle Sam? His exact origins are unknown, but it is thought that he was named after a man called Samuel Wilson. During the War of 1812, between Britain and the United States, he was a businessman who sold the US Army beef in barrels. The barrels were labelled 'US', which he said stood for 'Uncle Sam'. People then took up the

The 43 presidents of the United States have had more than 400 pets between them, including a bear, a tobacco-eating goat and even an elephant. There is even a Presidential Pet Museum!

Here are some of the more unusual pets that presidents had:

☞ The very first president, George Washington, had a parrot called Polly.

☞ Thomas Jefferson's pets included a mockingbird and two bear cubs.

☞ An alligator and silkworms were the strange pets of John Quincy Adams.

☞ Imagine keeping two tiger cubs, as President Martin Van Buren did.

☞ James Buchanan kept an eagle and an elephant!

☞ Abraham Lincoln loved his pets, which included a turkey, goats, ponies, cats, dogs, pigs and a white rabbit.

☞ Andrew Johnson had white mice.

☞ Ulysses S. Grant almost had a farm, with horses, pigs, dogs, a parrot and roosters.

☞ The next president, Rutherford B. Hayes, had cats, dogs, canaries, cows, horses and goats.

☞ The following president, Theodore Roosevelt, had

even more animals! He had a badger called Josiah, a pony called Algonquin, a macaw, a piebald rat called Jonathon and a garter snake called Emily Spinach. Then there were his 12 horses, five bears, five guinea pigs, several lizards, a flying squirrel and a raccoon. As if that wasn't enough, he also had a lion, a hyena and a zebra!

☞ Calvin Coolidge had a donkey called Ebeneezer, as well as a bear, an antelope, a hippopotamus and some lion cubs.

☞ John F. Kennedy was another president who loved his animals. He had lots of dogs, cats and hamsters.

☞ Jimmy Carter's pets were ordinary – a dog and a cat – but they had funny names: Grits and Misty Malarky Ying Yang!

☞ Bill Clinton's pets were pretty ordinary too – a Labrador and a cat – but the cat did have a strange name: Socks.

☞ Like his father, George H.W. Bush, who was President from 1989 to 1993, President George W. Bush has a Springer spaniel, who was born in the White House in 1989. He also has a Scottish terrier and a cat. His other cat now lives in California, because it was too wild to live in the White House.

idea that 'Uncle Sam' was a familiar name for the federal government. As recently as 1961 Congress passed a resolution that acknowledged Samuel Wilson as the inspiration for the symbol of Uncle Sam.

Sam Wilson looked nothing like the Uncle Sam described above. That Uncle Sam was an invention of political cartoonists, who wanted to portray him as a gentlemanly, wise old man. The most famous picture of Uncle Sam appeared on an army recruiting poster saying 'I WANT YOU' during the First World War.

That's entertainment

Tipping in bars and restaurants is essential in the USA. This is because waiters and waitresses are given very low wages, so they need their tips to live. Taxi drivers, hairdressers and porters are tipped, too.

Most Americans love to shop in big shopping malls or centres, which have car parks, restaurants and often cinemas as well as lots of different stores. There are around 50,000 shopping malls in the US and more are being built all the time. In 2003 more than 200 million adults visited a shopping centre each month in the USA!

The Mall of America in Minneapolis, Minnesota, is one of the largest indoor malls in the world. Funnily enough, it has another enormous shopping centre, the Southdale Center (as Americans spell it), just 15 minutes drive away. At the moment the world's biggest mall is in Edmonton in Canada, but there are many plans to build even larger malls in the US, where people still want things to be bigger, faster and better.

State to State – A Whistlestop Tour of the USA

All 50 states are listed on the top of the Lincoln Memorial as shown on the back of the five-dollar note: **Alabama, Alaska, Arizona, Arkansas, California, Colorado, Connecticut, Delaware, Florida, Georgia, Hawaii, Idaho, Illinois, Indiana, Iowa, Kansas, Kentucky, Louisiana, Maine, Maryland, Massachusetts, Michigan, Minnesota, Mississippi, Missouri, Montana, Nebraska, Nevada, New Hampshire, New Jersey, New Mexico, New York, North Carolina, North Dakota, Ohio, Oklahoma, Oregon, Pennsylvania, Rhode Island, South Carolina, South Dakota, Tennessee, Texas, Utah, Vermont, Virginia, Washington** (which is nowhere near Washington, DC!), **West Virginia, Wisconsin** and **Wyoming**.

As well as the 50 states, there are two more areas that are parts of the US: the District of Columbia, which contains the capital city, Washington; and the Commonwealth of Puerto Rico, an island with its own government that became US territory in 1898.

There are six regions and the fifty states in the USA each fall into one of the regions below. Here are some facts about the states that you might not know!

The Northeast
Connecticut
The state song is 'Yankee Doodle Dandy'.

The branding of farm animals in the United States began

in Connecticut when farmers were required by law to mark all their pigs.

In Hartford you may not, under any circumstances, cross the street walking on your hands!

Connecticut was home to the first beefburger (1895), the first Polaroid camera (1934), the first helicopter (1939) and the first commercially available colour televisions (1948).

Maine

About 40 million lbs/18 kgs (nearly 90 per cent) of the nation's lobster supply is caught off the coast of Maine.

Maine produces 99 per cent of all the blueberries in the country.

Massachusetts

Boston built the first subway system in the United States in 1897. Norfolk County is the birthplace of four US presidents: John Adams, John Quincy Adams, John Fitzgerald Kennedy and George Herbert Walker Bush.

New Hampshire

The first potato planted in the United States was put in the ground at Londonderry Common Field in 1719.

Alan Bartlett Shepard, Jr., the first American to travel in space, is from East Derry, New Hampshire.

Rhode Island

Rhode Island is the smallest state in the United States. It covers an area of just 1,214 square miles (3,144 square kilometres).

The first circus in the United States began putting on shows in Newport, Rhode Island in 1774.

Rhode Island was the last of the original 13 colonies to become a state.

Vermont

The name of the state comes from the French words *vert* ('green') and *mont* ('mountain').

Montpelier is the largest producer of maple syrup in the United States.

The Mid-Atlantic

Delaware

Delaware was the first state in the USA; it became a state on 7 December 1787, when it accepted the US Constitution.

Delaware even has a state drink – milk.

Finnish settlers arrived in Delaware in the mid-1600s and brought with them plans for the log cabin. One of their cabins has been preserved and is on display at the Delaware Agricultural Museum in Dover.

According to tradition, Betsy Ross's famous flag, the Stars and Stripes, was first flown at the Battle of Cooch's Bridge. This historic site is located on Route 4 in Newark.

The Blue Hen chicken is the official state bird. The hens were noted for their fighting ability. Delaware is sometimes referred to as the Blue Hen State.

Maryland

On 24 June 1784, in Baltimore, 13-year-old Edward Warren became airborne in the first successful manned balloon launch in the United States.

Ezra Cornell, the founder of Cornell University in Ithaca, New York, lived in Bladensburg and is said to have invented the telegraph pole.

New Jersey

New Jersey has the highest population density in the US, with an average 1,030 people per square mile, which is 13 times the national average.

In order to meet the increasing demand for his wire rope John Roebling opened a factory in Trenton, New Jersey, in 1848. Roebling, along with his two sons, Washington and Ferdinand, built a suspension bridge across the gorge of the Niagara River. They then built the Brooklyn Bridge in New York City, and many other suspension bridges in the United States.

New York

Dairying is New York's most important farming activity, with more than 18,000 farms 'upstate' (in the part of the state that isn't New York City).

Chittenago was the home of L. Frank Baum, author of *The Wizard of Oz*. It features yellow brick pavements leading to Auntie Em's and other Oz-themed businesses. Chittenago is the location of an annual Munchkins parade.

Oneida has the world's smallest church: it is just 3.5 feet (1.07 metres) by six feet (1.8 metres).

The first daily newspaper in Yiddish (Jewish) appeared in 1885 in New York City.

Pennsylvania

In 1909 the first baseball stadium was built in Pittsburgh.

Hershey is considered the 'Chocolate Capital of the United States', because it is the town where Hershey bars and other Hershey products are made.

Pennsylvania was the first state of the 50 in the United States to put the address of its website on its licence plates.

No US state produces more mushrooms than Pennsylvania.

The South

Alabama

Alabama workers built the first rocket to put humans on the Moon.

The saguaro cactus blossom is the official state flower. The white flower blooms on the tips of the desert plant during May and June. The saguaro is the largest American cactus.

Arkansas

William Jefferson Clinton was born in Hope on 19 August 1946. He was the 42nd US President, serving from 1993 to 2001.

The community of Mountain View is called the Folk Capital of America. The little town preserves the pioneer way of life and puts it on display for visitors at the Ozark Folk Center State Park from March to October.

Florida

Florida is known as the 'Sunshine State' because it normally has fine weather, though it is also famous for being regularly visited by hurricanes. Florida is not the southernmost state in the United States, though even many Americans think it is. Hawaii is further south.

Georgia

Georgia was named for King George II of England.

The pirate Edward 'Blackbeard' Teach made a home on what is now called Blackbeard Island. The US Congress made the island a protected wilderness area in 1975.

The official state fish is the largemouth bass.

In Gainesville, which calls itself the Chicken Capital of the World, it is illegal to eat chicken with a fork.

Kentucky

Cheeseburgers were first served in 1934 at Kaolin's Restaurant in Louisville.

The first Kentucky Fried Chicken restaurant, which used to be owned and operated by Colonel Sanders himself, is located in Corbin, Kentucky.

Louisiana

Louisiana was named in honour of King Louis XIV of France.

Louisiana is the only state in the union that does not have counties. Its political subdivisions are called parishes.

49

Louisiana is the only state with a large population of Cajuns, descendants of the French-speaking Acadians who were driven out of Canada in the 1700s because they wouldn't pledge allegiance to the British King.

Mississippi
The world's largest shrimp is on display at the Old Spanish Fort Museum in Pascagoula.

Missouri
Missouri's name is an Algonquin Indian term meaning 'river of the big canoes'.

Missouri is known as the 'Show Me State'. The expression may have begun in 1899, when Congressman Willard Duncan Vandiver stated, 'I'm from Missouri and you've got to show me.'

The first successful parachute jump to be made from a moving airplane was made by Captain Berry at St Louis in 1912.

At the St Louis World's Fair in 1904 Richard Blechyden served tea with ice and invented iced tea. The ice-cream cone was also invented at the World's Fair. An ice cream seller ran out of cups and asked a waffle vendor to help by rolling up waffles to hold ice cream.

North Carolina
Pepsi Cola was invented and first served in New Bern in 1898.

The Outer Banks of North Carolina host some of the most beautiful beaches in the country.

South Carolina
The walls of the American fort on Sullivan Island in Charleston Harbor were made of spongy Palmetto logs. This

was helpful in protecting the fort during the American Revolution, because the British cannonballs bounced off the logs.

Tennessee

Elvis Presley's home, Graceland, is located in Memphis. Graceland is the second most visited house in the country.

There are more horses per capita in Shelby County than in any other county in the United States.

Virginia

Virginia was named after England's 'Virgin Queen,' Elizabeth I.

Virginia has produced more US presidents than any other state. They include George Washington and Thomas Jefferson.

West Virginia

West Virginia's nickname is the 'Mountain State' and its motto is 'Mountaineers are always free'. It used to be part of Virginia, but its people were opposed to slavery and it broke away when most of Virginia decided to join the Confederacy during the Civil War.

Nearly 75 per cent of West Virginia is covered by forests.

The Midwest

Illinois

The world's first skyscraper was built in Chicago in 1885.

Chicago, the biggest city in Illinois and the centre of the Midwestern region, is home to the Chicago Bears American football team, the Chicago Blackhawks ice hockey team, the Chicago Bulls basketball team, the Chicago Cubs and Chicago Whitesox baseball teams, and the Chicago Fire soccer team.

Illinois is known as the 'Prairie State', probably because out of the Midwestern states that fill the Great Plains, or prairies, between the Appalachians and the Rockies, it is the one with the most people.

Indiana

The explorers Lewis and Clark set out from Fort Vincennes on their exploration of the Northwest Territory, the area of then unknown land that has since been divided up into several Midwestern states.

The first professional baseball game was played in Fort Wayne, Indiana, on 4 May 1871.

Iowa

The wild canary is the state bird of Iowa.

Quaker Oats, in Cedar Rapids, is the largest cereal company in the world.

Elk Horn in the largest Danish settlement in the USA.

Kansas

Kansas won the award for most beautiful licence plate for the wheat plate design issued in 1981.

At one time it was against the law to serve ice cream on cherry pie in Kansas.

The Kansas state animal is the buffalo.

Michigan

The name 'Michigan' comes from an Algonquian Chippewa word *meicigama*, which means 'big sea water' (referring to the Great Lakes).

Although Michigan is often called the 'Wolverine State', there are no longer any wolverines (members of the weasel family) in Michigan.

Minnesota

Minnesota has 90,000 miles of shoreline, more than California, Florida and Hawaii combined, even though it is far from both the Atlantic and the Pacific.

Minnesota has 22,000 rivers, ponds and wetlands, more than any other state except Texas and Alaska, thanks to the glaciers left behind from the snowy winters.

Nebraska

The Lied Jungle located in Omaha is the world's largest indoor rain forest.

Nebraska has the largest aquifer (underground lake/water supply) in the US, the Oglala aquifer.

Nebraska has more miles of river than any other state.

North Dakota

Dakota is the Sioux Indian word for 'friend.'

North Dakota grows more sunflowers than any other state. Milk is the official state beverage (it is also the state drink of 16 other states!).

Ohio

Cleveland boasts North America's first traffic light. It began operating on 5 August 1914.

Ermal Fraze invented the pop-top (easy-open) can in Kettering.

James J. Ritty of Dayton, Ohio, invented the cash register in 1879 to stop his patrons from pilfering house profits.

Akron was the first city to use police cars and Cincinnati had the first professional city fire department.

South Dakota

The sculptor Gutzon Borglum began drilling into Mount Rushmore in South Dakota in 1927. The creation of his 'Shrine to Democracy' took 14 years and cost him $1 million. Borglum carved the faces of four US presidents – George Washington, Thomas Jefferson, Theodore Roosevelt and Abraham Lincoln – into the mountain. But his son had to complete the Roosevelt carving when Borglum died in 1941.

Fossilised remains of life 50 million years ago have been arranged in unusual forms at Lemmon, the world's largest petrified wood park.

Wisconsin

Wisconsin has 7,446 streams and rivers.

End to end they'd stretch 26,767 miles (43,076 kilometres). That is more than enough to circle the globe at the equator.

Door County has five state parks and 250 miles (402 kilometres) of shoreline along Lake Michigan. These figures represent more than any other county in the country.

The Southwest

Arizona

Petrified wood is the official state fossil. Most petrified wood comes from the Petrified Forest in northeastern Arizona.

The palo verde is the official state tree. Its name means 'green stick' and it blooms a brilliant yellow-gold in April or May.

The cactus wren is the official state bird. It grows seven to eight inches long and likes to build nests in the protection of thorny desert plants, such as under the arms of the giant saguaro cactus.

New Mexico

Santa Fe is the highest capital city in the United States, at 7,000 feet (2,134 metres) above sea level.

Las Cruces makes the world's largest enchilada on the first weekend in October at the Whole Enchilada Fiesta.

Oklahoma

Oklahoma is one of only two states whose capital city's name includes the state name. The other is Indiana, whose capital is Indianapolis.

Oklahoma's state wild flower, the Indian blanket, is red with yellow tips. It symbolises the state's scenic beauty as well as its Indian (Native American) heritage. The wild flower blooms in June and July.

Texas

Texas is popularly known as the 'Lone Star State' because the symbol of the state, which used to be an independent republic, is a single white star.

The Alamo is located in San Antonio. It is where Texas defenders fell to Mexican General Santa Anna and the phrase 'Remember the Alamo' originated. The Alamo is the state's most popular historic site.

Texas is the only state to have had the flags of six different nations flying over it: Spain, France, Mexico, the Republic of Texas, the Confederate States during the Civil War and the United States. Texas was Spanish from 1519 to 1685, French from 1685 to 1690, Spanish again from 1690 to 1821, Mexican from 1821 to 1836, independent from 1836 to 1845, part of the United States from 1845 to 1861, and one of the Confederate States from 1861 to 1865, before being readmitted into the United States.

More wool comes from the state of Texas than any other state in the United States. Edwards Plateau in west central Texas is the top sheep-farming area in the country.

The West

Alaska

In 1867 US Secretary of State William H. Seward offered Russia $7,200,000, or two cents per acre, for Alaska, which was then called Russian America. Many Americans called the purchase 'Seward's Folly' because they thought he was stupid to buy what they thought was wasteland.

But Joe Juneau's discovery of gold in 1880 ushered in a gold rush era. The state capital, Juneau, was named in his honour. It is the only state capital with no roads leading in to it.

Colorado

The word 'Colorado' is Spanish for the colour red, and refers to the muddy Colorado River.

The Colorado town of Fountain has the distinction of being the most accurate representation of the American 'melting pot'. Fountain was chosen after a Queen's College sociologist found from Census Bureau statistics that it best represented the diverse population of the United States.

California

The name 'California' originally referred to a mythical Spanish island ruled by a queen called Califia, which was featured in a Spanish romance, *Las Sergas de Esplandian*, written by Garcia Ordonez de Montalvo in 1510. The Spanish explorers originally thought that California was an island.

California's nickname is the 'Golden State', referring to the Gold Rush that started in 1849 and attracted thousands of people to the territory, which had only recently been taken from Mexico. Its population now is nearly 34 million, making it the most populous of the 50 states.

Alpine County is the eighth-smallest of California's 58 counties. It has no high school, ATMs (cash machines), dentists, banks or traffic lights.

Hawaii

The state of Hawaii is made up of more than 130 islands, including eight main islands: Niihau, Kauai, Oahu, Maui, Molokai, Lanai, Kahoolawe and the Big Island of Hawaii. From east to west Hawaii is the widest state in the United States.

Hawaii is the 50th state in the USA; it became a state on 21 August 1959.

The flag of Hawaii was commissioned by King Kamehameha I of Hawaii in 1816. The king had unified the islands of Hawaii in 1810, using a schooner armed with a cannon. Before that time each of the main islands had been a separate kingdom. The eight stripes of white, red and blue represent the eight main islands. The Union Jack is in the upper left corner of Hawaii's flag, honouring Hawaii's long relationship with the British.

Hawaii is the only state that grows coffee, and more than one third of the world's commercial supply of pineapples comes from Hawaii.

Idaho

In Idaho a state law forbids citizens giving other citizens any box of candy (sweets) that weighs more than 50 lbs/22.7kgs. Idaho is famous for its potatoes. The most famous potatoes were planted here in 1836. Today one-third of the country's potatoes are grown in Idaho.

Montana

The average square mile of land in Montana contains 1.4 elk, 1.4 pronghorn antelope and 3.3 deer.

At the Rocky Mountain Front Eagle Migration Area, west of the city of Great Falls, more golden eagles have been seen in a single day than anywhere else in the country.

At Bowdoin National Wildlife Refuge it is possible to see up to 1,700 nesting pelicans.

Nevada

In the desert Death Valley the kangaroo rat can live its entire life without drinking a drop of liquid.

The ghost town of Rhyolite still honours the early pioneers and their dreams. Remains of the train depot, glass house, bank and other buildings are on display.

Oregon

Oregon has more ghost towns than any other state.

The Columbia River gorge is considered by many to be the best place in the world for windsurfing.

Utah

The completion of the world's first transcontinental railway was celebrated at Promontory in Utah, where the Central Pacific and Union Pacific Railroads met on 10 May 1869. The spot is now known as Golden Spike National Historic Site.

The Great Salt Lake covers 2,100 square miles (5,440 square kilometres), with an average depth of 13 feet (four metres). The deepest point is 34 feet (10.4 metres).

The average snowfall in the mountains near Salt Lake City is 500 inches (1,260 centimetres). Because of the state's inland location Utah's snow is unusually dry, earning it the reputation of having the world's greatest powder snow. Fourteen Alpine ski resorts operate in Utah.

Washington State

Washington State produces more apples than any other state in the union.

This state has more glaciers than the other 47 states of the continental US (the USA minus Alaska and Hawaii) combined.

Everett is the site of the world's largest building, Boeing's final assembly plant, where the 747, 767 and 777 aircraft are put together.

Medina is the home of the world's wealthiest man, Bill Gates, the founder and head of Microsoft.

Wyoming

'Wyoming' is an Algonquin Indian word meaning 'large prairie place'. The state has two nicknames: the 'Equality State' and the 'Cowboy State'.

Wyoming was the first state to give women the right to vote.

A School Day in the USA

There are some differences between American schools and those in Great Britain or Ireland. You might think American children are lucky because they usually do not have to wear uniforms. Only those who go to some private and Catholic schools must do so.

At the age of six, or sometimes five, children usually go to elementary school moving up a grade, (from one to eight) each year. But in some places in the US children go to middle or junior school (grade five to eight). High schools have grades from nine to 12. The youngest, 9th graders, are called freshmen, 10th graders are called sophomores, 11th graders are known as juniors and 12th graders are called seniors. Confused?!

In the US, there are hardly any schools that just boys or girls attend. Some states have their own rules about education. For example, most schools in the country say children must go to school until they are 16, but in some states you must stay until you are 18!

The subjects taught in elementary schools are pretty much the same as in the UK. After that in most states, children must take science, math(s), English and reading or language, arts and history. There are some differences between the

UK	US
glue	gum
rubber	eraser
maths	math [without 's']
holiday	vacation
school dinner	hot lunch
staff room	teachers' lounge
mucking about	off task
drawing pins	pushpins or thumbtacks

states so that if you are in the 8th grade in Idaho for example, you must take classes in health and physical education.

Girls and boys play sports – like football, basketball, tennis, soccer, and golf – separately. Boys can sometimes also do wrestling and baseball. Girls can choose to do volleyball, basketball, softball, or to be a cheerleader.

Easter, summer and Christmas school holidays in the United States are the same as in the UK (although in the states they would say 'happy holidays' rather than 'happy Christmas'. But there are also some different holidays (which they call vacations), like Labour Day, Thanksgiving and Martin Luther King Day.

Some of the best things about

NEw yORK CiTY

according to
Ethan Simmons,
aged 10,
of Selina,
Kansas

YANKEE STADIUM

"When we saw a Yankees baseball game it was an amazing buzz"

CONEY ISLAND

CYCLONE

"Imagine an amusement park as big as a town!"

CENTRAL PARK

"It goes on, like, forever"

BROOKLYN BRIDGE

"The view you get is amazing. It's like driving to another planet"

SKYSCRAPERS

"It would be so great to live in one"

STREET LIFE

"It's exciting just walking around"

THE MUSEUM OF MODERN ART

"They've got tons of really wild pictures in there"

TIMES SQUARE

"On New Year's Eve they have a humongous outdoor party"

Ethan's overall verdict on New York?
"I want to live there one day – maybe in TriBeCa or Williamsburg. They're the coolest areas"

Fabulous Buildings, Sights and National Parks

Four great national parks

The US has the world's oldest system for creating and protecting national parks, nature reserves and historic monuments, and there are also many sights to see in every major city. Here are four of the best:

Yellowstone was the world's very first national park. It is in three states – Wyoming, Montana and Idaho. It contains mountains, hot springs, bears, moose and 200 kinds of birds, and it forms one of the world's largest wildlife sanctuaries.

Glacier Park is an area in the mountains of Montana, near the border with Canada, with glaciers, lakes, wild flowers, forests, waterfalls and wildlife.

Mammoth Cave National Park in central Kentucky contains the longest cave system in the world: five separate levels of caves stretch for more than 345 miles (555 kilometres)! They were formed by eroded limestone and contain a mummified body of a man that dates from pre-Columbian times (before 1492). Native Americans once lived in the caves, but you probably wouldn't want to, as you might have to share them with bats, insects and eyeless fish!

Yosemite National Park, in the Sierra Nevada

mountains of California, forms a huge valley with cliffs, pinnacles, peaks and waterfalls.

In New York City

The Empire State Building is one of the most famous buildings in the USA. When it was built in 1931 it was the tallest building in the world, at 436 feet (145 metres) high. But what made the people who built it so clever was that it took them only 410 days to finish it! Even today they hold the record for the fastest construction of a major skyscraper. Of course, the top of this building was shown in the famous film *King Kong* and many tourists go up there for great views of New York City.

There's lots more to see in New York, including:

☞ The Guggenheim Museum, designed like a massive snail by Frank Lloyd Wright and full of wonderful modern art.

The Guggenheim Museum, New York

☞ Brooklyn Bridge, which, when it was completed in 1883, was the world's longest suspension bridge and the tallest structure in the city.

☞ The Chrysler Building, probably the city's most beautiful building, with a stainless steel tower and gargoyles.

☞ Ellis Island, where between 1892 and 1954 more than 17 million men, women and children arrived in the USA from Europe, to become the ancestors of 40 per cent of people living in the US today.

☞ The Statue of Liberty, given to the United States by France in the 19th century and shipped in pieces across the Atlantic Ocean, to commemorate the alliance of France with the American colonies during the American Revolution.

☞ 'Ground Zero', the place where, on 11 September 2001, the city's skyline was changed forever when the Twin Towers of the World Trade Center were destroyed in terrorist attacks – in 2003 it was decided that the site should be redeveloped and Daniel Libeskind was chosen to lead the design team.

☞ Wall Street, today the centre of the country's financial system, but a few hundred years ago the site of a wall that the Dutch built to keep the Native Americans out.

Niagara Falls

Every year 12 million people go to the border with Canada to see the second-biggest waterfalls in the world. There have been a number of crazy daredevils over the years who have gone down these enormous, powerful waterfalls in different contraptions. Most have survived, but not all of them! The most famous stunt was performed by a Frenchman, Jean-François Gravelot, who crossed the Niagara Falls on a tightrope in 1859.

Independence Hall in Philadelphia

This hall was built as the colony's State House, the headquarters of its government, way back in 1732. It is important because it is where the US Declaration of Independence was signed on 4 July 1776 and where the United States made itself independent from Great Britain. The Liberty Bell is nearby, which was first rung on that day.

The Great Smoky Mountains

These mountains are the highest points in the state of Tennessee. They are part of a national park that is 95 per cent forest. Nearly 10 million people come here every year to enjoy the beautiful scenery, with black bears, lots of birds and waterfalls. It's the most visited national park in the United States. Its name refers to the smoke-like bluish haze that often envelops these fabled mountains.

In Washington, DC

The most famous home in the USA is the White House, which is, of course, the residence of the President of the United States. It was actually designed by an Irish-born architect, James Hoban, at the end of the 18th century, when the city was being made into the new country's capital and a

memorial to its first President, George Washington.

The Lincoln Memorial has 36 columns, to represent the number of states in the United States at the time of President Abraham Lincoln's death. The Jefferson Memorial honours the third President, Thomas Jefferson. He wrote the Declaration of Independence, invented the US dollar, doubled the size of the country by buying land previously owned by the French, and started the Library of Congress, which is now the biggest library in the world.

The Cathedral Caverns

This national park in Alabama has what is believed to be the largest stalagmite, named Goliath, as well as the largest cave opening and cavern room in the world.

In Florida

Everglades National Park is an area of wetlands in Florida, with mangroves and swamps as well as lots of pink flamingos and other birds, special wild flowers, such as orchids, and rare wildlife, such as Florida panthers and the dolphin-like manatee. It is also the only place in the whole of the United States where crocodiles live!

At the John F. Kennedy Space Center at Cape Canaveral, on Florida's east coast, you can get to know the story of NASA's exploration of space. There is a full-size replica of the space shuttle Explorer and you can walk through a giant model of a module from the new International Space Station. Visitors can watch films about the planet Mars and the Pathfinder exploration, see real rockets, and go to the Apollo/Saturn Center, which is home to lots of things from the historic moon landings.

Did you know that there are two real Disney towns in Florida, called Celebration and Seaside? They were built in the past 10 years for people who want to live in small, clean and tidy towns where everyone knows their neighbours!

The Sears Tower

This skyscraper in Chicago, Illinois, has 110 storeys and is the highest building in the country. It is eight storeys higher than the Empire State Building, which used to

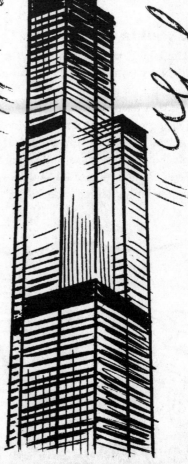

73

be America's highest building. The Sears Tower is the only building in the USA that has its own ZIP code (post code). From the sky deck at the top you can see four states – Illinois, Indiana, Wisconsin and Michigan. The tower has enough steel to build 50,000 cars. You might wonder how they clean the 16,000 windows: they have six washing machines on the roof!

Cahokia Mounds

These large pyramid mounds form more than 80 earthworks by Native Americans in southwestern Illinois. Cahokia was founded around the year 700. There were once more than 120 mounds here. Now 68 of them are preserved in a park area. During pre-Columbian times (before Christopher Columbus arrived) it was for a while the largest North American city north of central Mexico. The largest mound is called the Monk's Mound, and it's enormous – 100 feet (about 30 metres) high, with a base 790 feet (about 235 metres) around!

An excavation here found the burial site of an important ruler, a man in his 40s. He had been buried on a bed of more than 20,000 seashells arranged in the shape of a bird as birds were very important to the people who lived in this area.

In Colorado

The Grand Canyon is one of the most important natural wonders. One mile (1.6 kilometres) deep, 277 miles (446 kilometres) long and up to 18 miles (29 kilometres) wide, it is just so amazing that it is hard to describe in words. It was formed by the cutting action of the Colorado River over five million years.

Mesa Verde National Park, in southwestern Colorado, contains the best-preserved cliff houses in the United States.They were built in shallow caves along canyon walls from the sixth to the 14th centuries by ancient Pueblo Native Americans who lived here. Three of them are open to the public: Spruce Tree House, Balcony House and Cliff Palace.

The bridge that stands highest over water anywhere in the world is the Royal Gorge Bridge over the Arkansas River in Colorado. Built in 1929 for $350,000, it spans 1,053 feet (321 metres) above the water.

In New Mexico

Chaco Culture National Historical Park was (between 850 and 1250) a major centre for ceremonies and trade for prehistoric Native American people. It is special because they were very clever in the way they constructed marvellous buildings, roads, dams and other things using sophisticated engineering. Even 1,000 years later they seem amazing. It is also special because it is part of the sacred homeland of several groups of Native Americans: the Pueblo peoples of New Mexico, the Hopi of Arizona and the Navajo of the Southwest.

Taos Pueblos is an ancient town in New Mexico where

around 2,000 Pueblo Native Americans live in adobe (mud) buildings. In the early 17th century the town became the headquarters of the Spanish mission, bringing Christianity to the Native Americans, and these ancient communal dwellings are seen as architectural masterpieces.

Las Vegas, Nevada

Some people say that Las Vegas is the biggest theme park for adults in the world. But just 80 or so years ago the city was just dust in the desert. It was literally built out of nothing – there were no roads, no buildings and no people there. Today more than one million people live there and 35 million more visit on holiday each year from all over the world.

Although most people come for the casinos, there is also 'The Strip', which is a kind of Disneyland of hotels and bright lights. Here you can see the world in miniature – copies of the Egyptian Pyramids, the New York skyline, the Statue of Liberty, a full-scale pirate battle, and a bubbling volcano.

In Arizona

Petrified Forest National Park isn't a frightened forest! It's a national park in northeastern Arizona with fossilised trees that are 225 million years old – some of dinosaurs. Soldiers from the US Army found this area in the mid-1800s and told amazing stories of a 'painted desert with trees turned to stone'. When trees become petrified it is almost as if they turn to stone. Giant redwood trees became buried in volcanic ash and water. The pressure, the lack of oxygen and sunlight, and the silica in the ash turning to quartz caused the wood to become like rock. In time, the wind and erosion exposed them, and you can see them today.

The largest meteorite crater in the world is in Winslow, Arizona. It is 4,150 feet (1,265 metres) across and 150 feet (nearly 46 metres) deep.

Remember the nursery rhyme about London Bridge falling down? Well, in the late 1960s the old London Bridge actually was falling down! Built in 1831, it was the victim of its own immense weight and was sinking into the clay of the River Thames. When a rich American called Robert McCulloch said that he wanted to bring the 140-year-old London Bridge to Lake Havasu in the Arizona desert,

people laughed. But he bought the falling-down bridge for $2.4 million, which at the time was the highest price ever paid for an antique. The bridge had to be taken apart brick by brick, which took three years! The bricks were then flown to the US and it was put back together. Today it is a big attraction and it has made the town grow. (Some people say that Mr McCulloch thought he was buying Tower Bridge, but that was just a joke that Londoners made up.)

The Rainbow Bridge

The world's largest natural bridge (made of rock) is the Rainbow Bridge, hidden away in the remote canyons at the

bottom of Navajo Mountain in the state of Utah. From its base to the top of the arch, it reaches 290 feet (88.4 metres), nearly the height of the Statue of Liberty, and spans 275 feet (83.8 metres) across the river.

In San Francisco

San Francisco, on the coast of California, developed at the time of the Gold Rush in the 1850s, but was almost completely destroyed by an earthquake in 1906. Since then it has been rebuilt to become one of the most visited cities in the USA, with sights that include:

☞ The cable cars, which still run the same way they did in 1873, propelled by huge loops of steel over the steep hills of the city.

☞ Coit Tower, a 210 feet (64 metres) tall Art Deco tower built in 1933, giving 360-degree views of the city and bay.

☞ Lombard Street, which is said to be the 'crookedest street in the world', with eight switchbacks.

☞ But the symbol of the city is the Golden Gate Bridge on San Francisco Bay. It isn't gold: it is painted a colour called international orange, so that it stands out from the blue of the sea and sky, which makes it easy for ships to see it even in the mist. Its name comes from Golden

Gate Strait, at the entrance to San Francisco Bay from the Pacific Ocean. When it was opened in 1937 it had the longest span in the world, a record it kept until 1964; today it has the seventh-longest span. The steel wires used in its cables are long enough to circle the Earth three times.

Scary prison, great food

On an island near the city of San Francisco is the famous prison of Alcatraz. Between 1933 and 1963 many of the most dangerous American criminals, such as Al 'Scarface' Capone, Alvin 'Creepy' Karpis and George 'Machine Gun' Kelly, were put here because it was so hard to escape from. More than 300 people who worked at the prison lived on the island. They included around 60 children, who had their very own bowling alley and soda fountain in the prison grounds. They had a good journey to school too – they took the ferry to San Francisco. Today the prison is a museum.

Redwoods and giant sequoias

The tallest tree in the world is a California redwood known as Tall Tree, which was measured at nearly 368 feet (112 metres) tall. The biggest tree in the world is a giant sequoia, the General Sherman Tree, which measures nearly 102 feet (31 metres) around its trunk. Both these kinds of trees get to be so big partly because they live so long — California redwoods can live for more than 2,000 years and giant sequoias can live for more than 3,500 years. Also, because their trunks are so thick they don't burn down easily in forest fires. Redwood National Park on the Pacific coast, in northwestern California, features seals, sea lions and birds as well as giant redwoods. Muir Woods, on Highway 101, near San Francisco, also has some giant redwoods.

The world's most famous pavement

Where else but in Hollywood can you stand on top of Elvis Presley, Marilyn Monroe and James Dean? The Hollywood Walk of Fame is a pavement along Hollywood Boulevard and Vine Street with more than 2,000 stars embedded in it. It is a way of honouring famous people in show business.

Marilyn Monroe

Elvis Presley's star can be found outside the Hollywood Wax Museum, Marilyn Monroe's is in front of a branch of McDonald's, and James Dean's is right on the corner of Hollywood Boulevard and Vine Street. You can only dream of ever getting your own star, but if you live in Hollywood you can adopt your favourite star. It does mean, though, that you have to promise to polish it on the first Saturday of each month.

Crater Lake, Oregon

This is the deepest lake in the United States and the seventh-deepest in the world. It is a peaceful place with blue water, but it had a violent creation. Nearly 8,000 years ago a volcano called Mount Mazama erupted and collapsed in on itself. When the volcanic lava cooled, the enormous crater filled with rain and snow, and the lake was formed.

Glacier Bay

This bay forms a National Park near Juneau in Alaska. The glaciers falling from towering snow-covered mountains create spectacular displays of ice. The most famous is Muir Glacier, which is around two miles (3.2 kilometres) wide! Bears, deer, mountain goats and whales live in the park.

Hawaii's volcanoes

Two of the most dangerous volcanoes in the world are on the islands of Hawaii. Kilauea is the world's most active volcano and has a pit of fire. Mauna Loa, at nearly 14,000 feet (4,300 metres) high, is the biggest volcano on the planet and has an active crater on its top. They both took 70 million years to form!

Famous Inventors, Scientists and Artists

The real Pocahontas

Everyone knows the Disney film about the Indian girl, but there was a real person called Pocahontas. She was the daughter of an important chief of the Algonquian people in Virginia. Her real name was Matoaka: 'Pocahontas' was a nickname meaning 'the little playful one'.

Pocahontas did many things to try to make peace between the Native Americans and the English colonists. It is thought that she saved the life of the Englishman Captain John Smith, the governor of Virginia. In 1608 Pocahontas helped to free some Algonquian prisoners held by the colonists when she was only about 12 years old! She even became a Christian and married a colonist. Sadly she died in England at the age of just 22. (Her tomb can still be seen at Gravesend in Kent.)

Fit for a king

Hawaii is the only American state that was once ruled by a native king. King Kamehameha I, who was born around

1740, was the head of a family that ruled the Hawaiian islands for more than 100 years. A priest warned that Kamehameha would be a rebel, so his grandfather ordered that he be put to death. Luckily, other priests hid him and saved his life. He later became king and was very successful in battles, managing to unite all the different Hawaiian islands. His sons later became Kamehameha II and Kamehameha III.

A bestseller

Noah Webster was born in Connecticut in 1758 and lived during the time of George Washington. He was a teacher in a school in a shack and then became a lawyer. He wrote a spelling book that sold more than 100 million copies and wrote what he called 'American books for American children'. His textbooks were used in schools for nearly 100 years. Webster saw that the people in the new United States spoke many languages and often could not understand each other. He thought that there needed to be one 'mother tongue' for all Americans, so he wrote a dictionary for the people. He even travelled to Europe and learned other languages to help him to understand the origin of words.

Webster's American Dictionary of the English Language created a new standard, so that even today many words are spelled differently in the US than in other English-speaking countries: for example, 'center', 'color', 'kilometer', 'license plate', 'traveler'. Webster's dictionary sold more copies than any book in the United States except the Bible, and different versions of it can still be bought today.

A cut above the rest

Cyrus McCormick, born in 1809, grew up on a farm in Virginia. By the time he died, in 1884, he had earned millions of dollars and become one of the richest men in the country.

He had invented a reaping machine with a revolving blade to harvest wheat. Some said that it looked like a cross between a flying machine and a wheelbarrow. This completely changed the way people farmed. Before McCormick's reaping machine became common, a farmer could harvest only half an acre a day using a scythe, which is a big curved blade. With the new invention a farmer and a helper could harvest 12 acres a day!

McCormick also helped to change the lives of working people in the cities, starting in Chicago, where he set up a factory to make his machines. Until then, most tools and machines were made by hand. McCormick invented machines that could make machines, so that each one was identical, and they could all be easily repaired when they broke down, simply by replacing a broken part with a new one. Because of this McCormick is now known both as the 'father of modern agriculture' and as one of the pioneers of mass production.

America's funniest man?

Mark Twain was born in 1835 and grew up by the Mississippi River. He became a journalist and lecturer who travelled the world, and was often very funny. His most famous books are *The Adventures of Tom Sawyer* and *The Adventures of Huckleberry Finn*. He went to exotic places such as Hawaii (which at that time was called the Sandwich Islands) and Egypt. He often made fun of rich people, including the British royal family, and wrote what is called satire. He wrote *A Connecticut Yankee in King Arthur's Court*, about a man who travels back to the time of King Arthur. Here are a couple of Mark Twain's more famous lines:

☞ 'Always obey your parents when they are present.' (from 'Advice to Youth')

☞ 'Man is the only animal that blushes. Or needs to.' (from *Following the Equator*)

The man who didn't go to school

Thomas Alva Edison was probably the world's greatest inventor: he came up with more than 1,000 inventions. When he was a boy he was always asking questions. Once he even tried to hatch some eggs by sitting on them! His teacher thought he was stupid, so he only went to school for three months in his whole life.

Edison invented the light bulb and a cement mixer, but his favourite invention was the phonograph. When he was trying to improve the telegraph and the telephone, Edison found a way to record sound on tinfoil-coated cylinders. In 1877 he made a machine with two needles, one for recording and one for playback. 'Mary had a little lamb' were the first words that Edison recorded on the phonograph. Can you imagine how excited he was when he heard the machine play his words back to him? Since then the phonograph and the machines developed from it – the record player and the CD player – have made a lot of people very happy. In 1917, when the USA became involved in the First World War, Thomas Edison's company created a special version of the phonograph for the army, which was smaller and cheaper. The army bought lots of these so that the soldiers could listen to music from home to cheer them up.

Edison didn't give up inventing even after the phonograph made him rich. In 1888 he said: 'I am experimenting upon an instrument which does for the eye what the phonograph does for the ear.' The result of his experiments was the Kinematograph, the first movie camera. The very first film in the world is of someone who worked for Edison, Fred Ott, pretending to sneeze. Edison then made another film of two cats fighting in a boxing ring!

The real McCoy

You have probably heard the expression 'the real McCoy', which means 'the real thing'. But do you know where it came from? Elijah McCoy was born in Canada as the son of slaves who had run away from Kentucky. He was educated in Scotland, but returned to the US to live in Detroit in Michigan. Although he was a trained engineer, because of racism the only job available to him was that of a train fire/oil man, shovelling coal into the train's engine and lubricating the engine. McCoy studied how the train engine worked and in the 1870s he invented something called a lubricator, which oiled train wheels while the train was moving. He was one of the most important African-American inventors of his time – he obtained more than 50 patents between 1872 and 1929, even though he died penniless. He always used the highest standards of materials and workmanship, but many people tried to copy him. So people used the phrase 'the real McCoy' to mean the original high-quality machine, not the cheaper but lower-quality copy.

Early MTV

The first music videos started in the 90s – the 1890s, that is. A man called George Thomas first put music together with pictures. These were the ancestors of MTV and became a craze across the country by 1900. George Thomas got people to sing a song called 'The Little Lost Child' and took photos that were then printed on glass slides and painted in with colour. Musicians played music and the pictures were projected onto a screen. But on the first showing it all went wrong, with the pictures appearing upside down, and the audience roared with laughter. However, the song became a hit and 10,000 theatres across the country were soon showing illustrated songs. The music publishers loved it because they made so much money using the songs to sell sheet music to people who played songs in their houses.

Buffalo Bill

William Frederick Cody (1846–1917), known as Buffalo Bill, was a buffalo hunter and a US Army scout, but he gave up fighting to go into show business. He is probably best known as the man who gave the 'Wild West' its name. He produced a colourful theatre show called 'Buffalo Bill's Wild West and Congress of Rough Riders of the World', which became popular all over the world and helped to create the lasting image of the American West. Every time children play Cowboys and Indians they are paying tribute to Buffalo Bill, whose shows featured the first real Native Americans most people outside the West had ever seen.

Will you be my teddy bear?

Theodore Roosevelt was the 26th president of the United States. He was often called 'Teddy' for short and he is the person who gave the teddy bear its name. In 1902 Roosevelt went on a bear hunt in Mississippi. When he found a baby bear hit over the head with a club and tied to a tree by a guide, he asked for it to be killed to put it out of its misery. An American newspaper, the Washington Post, showed a cartoon about what had happened. The story became so popular that in less than a year the cartoon bear had become a toy for children called the teddy bear. A couple who owned a toy shop made two stuffed bears and wrote to Roosevelt asking if they could use the name 'Teddy's bear'. The rest is, as they say, history.

Magnificent men and their flying machine

People have always wanted to fly, but the US Army had tried so hard to build an airplane and failed that in 1903 the *New York Times* wrote that maybe in one million to 10 million years people might be able to make a plane that would fly. But two brothers called Wilbur and Orville Wright proved the paper wrong. They tested early theories about flight with balloons and kites, studied wind patterns, and tried different shapes of gliders. Then they studied how birds flew. They noticed that birds soared high into the wind and changed the shape of their wings to turn. They decided to use this technique to gain control in the air. Their very first flight was in 1903, for just 12 seconds, but then in 1904 they flew for five minutes. In 1911 their plane was the very first to cross the United States – in 84 days – but the plane crash-landed so many times that hardly any of the original construction was left when it arrived in California. The plane was called the 'Vin Fiz', after a fizzy grape-flavoured drink. The first plane they flew, the 'Kitty Hawk', was put in the Science Museum in London in 1928. Twenty years later it was sent back to the United States, and it can now be seen at the National Air Museum in Washington, DC.

It's magic!

Harry Houdini was a Hungarian Jew who went to live in the USA. He was one of the greatest magicians of all time, and amazed audiences in both Europe and North America. Houdini got bored with doing normal magic tricks and decided to do mainly escapes. In 1908, in St Louis, Missouri, Houdini introduced his escape from a giant milk can filled with water. It became a very popular trick and he took it on tour throughout the US, Britain and Germany. He once made an elephant called Jennie disappear. In 1913 he got into an 'Upside Down Water Torture Cell': his ankles were tied and he was put under water, upside down, and locked in, but he managed to get himself free. (Don't try this trick at home!) Houdini died on Halloween, but he did not die during an underwater escape as shown in the film *Houdini* (1953).

Walt and Mickey and Donald and...

Walt Disney's cartoons are still some of the best ever made. This is because Disney was always trying to get his animators to improve their drawings and to make their characters more lifelike. Not only was Disney a really good artist, but he was something of a genius too. The only other people who had done this before were the people who had created Popeye the Sailor Man and Felix the Cat.

Walt Disney first became famous with short films about Mickey Mouse, Donald Duck and other characters that he made up himself, but the longer and more famous Disney films are almost always taken from popular fairytales.

Amelia Earhart flies across the Atlantic

On 17 June 1928 Amelia Earhart became the first woman passenger to fly across the Atlantic Ocean in a plane called 'Friendship', with co-pilots Wilmer 'Bill' Stultz and Louis 'Slim' Gordon. The plane landed in South Wales with only a small amount of fuel left. Today planes carrying passengers cross the Atlantic in about seven hours, but Earhart's first trip across the Atlantic took more than 20 hours! It made her famous around the world. Earhart then became the first woman to fly alone across the Atlantic and then later across the eastern Pacific from Honolulu in Hawaii to Oakland in California.

She also broke lots of speed records. As well as being a great pilot, Earhart was a good writer, poet, photographer and teacher, and campaigned for women's rights. She disappeared while flying the Pacific in 1937.

The power of photographs

Dorothy Lange was a photographer who took pictures of ordinary people. Her most famous photograph, 'Migrant Mother', was taken in 1936. It shows a woman working in pea fields in California. She was a widow with seven children. This was the time of the Great Depression, when there was very little work and a lot of people were having trouble getting enough food. Her children managed to stay alive by eating frozen peas and birds they caught. Although she was only 32, the woman looks much older. The photograph was important because it showed people in the rest of the country what was happening and it brought money to the camp where the woman lived.

Satchmo!

Daniel Louis Armstrong (1901–71) was a great jazz trumpeter, composer and singer. He was nicknamed 'Satchmo' because people said that his mouth looked like a satchel. Armstrong was born in New Orleans, Louisiana, and soon became a well-known cornet player in clubs and on riverboats along the Mississippi River. He became world-famous for his incredible musical talent, especially his improvised solos. Armstrong also sang 'scat', a style in which nonsense words are used instead of real words. (Ella Fitzgerald also became famous for using scat in songs.) But there is no scat in Satchmo's most famous song, 'What a Wonderful World'.

A good plan

George Marshall was a soldier, but most people remember him for what he did in peacetime. Marshall held important positions in the US Army in both world wars, but later became Secretary of State and came up with the 'Marshall Plan'. This brought hope to many countries in Europe that were in ruins after the war and $13 billion to help them rebuild. Marshall received the Nobel Peace Prize in 1953 in recognition of his great achievement.

Jackson Pollock

As a painter Pollock had a very unusual style. He didn't use an easel or a palette, but put a huge canvas on the floor so that he could work on it from all sides. He felt that this gave him more freedom and that he could break the limits of traditional painting. Although a lot of critics praised him, many people didn't and still don't understand his style. In 1956 Time magazine called him 'Jack the Dripper' because of the way that he threw paint at the canvas, but he didn't really care about what anyone else thought. Pollock's paintings are examples of what is known as 'abstract expressionism'. It was the first important school of American painting to declare its independence from European styles and to influence art in other countries.

Jonas Salk

Until the 1950s polio was a common disease all over the world. It affected mostly children. Some adults got polio too, including Franklin Roosevelt, who was left permanently without the use of his legs in 1921, though he managed to serve 12 years as US President (1933 to 1945, longer than any other president) while keeping his condition secret. So scientists were racing to find a vaccine.

Jonas Salk, a son of Polish Jewish immigrants, worked with the US Army creating a flu vaccine. He then developed the polio vaccine and vaccinated more than one million children in the US aged between six and nine. Salk died in 1995, while searching for a vaccine for HIV/AIDS.

'Lazy Bones'

Can you imagine the days before remote controls for televisions? Around 50 years ago the Germans had used remote controls in the First World War, when they used radio-controlled motor boats to ram enemy ships, and in the 1940s American scientists developed similar controls to open garage doors. Radio-controlled bombs were then used in the Second World War. But it was only in 1950 that the first TV remote control, called 'Lazy Bones', was made. It was attached to the television set with a big wire, which was easy to trip over! In 1955 someone called Eugene Polley invented the 'Flashmatic', a wireless remote which was triggered by light. The problem was that on sunny days the sunlight could change channels! The next year Dr Robert Adler used

95

ultrasound waves in a new kind of remote control. Over nine million ultrasonic remote controls were sold. Infrared devices replaced ultrasonic remote controls in the early 1980s. Infrared works by using a light beam at such a low frequency that the human eye cannot see it. Today it is used for videos, CD players and DVD players.

Toy story

The Barbie doll was invented in 1959 by Ruth Handler, whose own daughter was called Barbara. The Ken doll was named after Ruth's son. Barbie is now one of the most popular dolls in the world. Every second of every day two Barbie dolls are sold somewhere in the world. The full name of Barbie is 'Barbie Millicent Roberts'. She is from Willows, Wisconsin, and went to Willows High School. Barbie has had more than 80 careers – everything from a rock star to a presidential candidate. The first Olympic-Athlete Barbie was introduced in 1975 and she represented an astronaut in 1965, 1986 and 1994. Did you know that Barbie has five sisters, Skipper, introduced in 1964, Tutti, a twin introduced in 1966, Stacie in 1992, Kelly in 1995 and Krissy in 1999?

Andy Warhol

The Pittsburgh-bred son of immigrants from Slovakia, Andy Warhol was an artist who used well-known images in his work because he saw how important they were in everyday life in the United States. He loved to use pictures of Mickey Mouse, which he saw as one of the most famous images of all time. He also used Howdy Doody, a ventriloquist's dummy from a 1950s television programme, and Father Christmas. He is most famous for his coloured pictures of Campbell's soup tins and Marilyn Monroe. Most people remember Andy Warhol for saying: 'In the future everybody will be world famous for 15 minutes.'

Food and Drink

Traditional foods

Wherever you go in America you will
find a vast range of different types of
food and restaurants. The choice of food is
astonishing. A lot of food eaten in
America came from Europe with the first
people who emigrated there to live and make a new life.
Dishes were often adapted to make use of local ingredients.
Michigan, for example, produces around three quarters of
the cherries grown in the United States, so people in this
state eat lots of cherry pie!

Traditional American dishes are fried chicken, meatloaf and
baked beans. But different states have different foods depending
on local tradition and produce. In the northeast, the dishes were
influenced by the English settlers. Southern cooking is quite
African. The New Orleans area has Cajun cooking which is a
spicy mixture of Spanish, French and African styles. In
California people use lots of fresh fruits and vegetables as well
as Asian, Mexican and Spanish flavours.

Southern food

Lots of vegetables are grown in the South of the United
States, and fish, oysters and crabs fill the waters. Around 150
years ago, most of the richest people in the USA lived in the
South and they really enjoyed their food. For just a normal
meal, they might have eaten veal pie, goose, trifle and ice

cream, with lots of other dishes.

Creole and Cajun cooking come from southern Louisiana. Creole is food from the city of New Orleans and Cajun comes from the countryside. Creole cooking is usually more sophisticated, with lots of sauces, and Cajun is often very spicy. Both kinds use many of the same foods, and have been affected by Native American, French, African-American and Spanish cooking.

Food served in the South is different depending on where exactly you are. Red beans and rice in Louisiana would be peas and rice in South Carolina. In the states of Virginia and Maryland crabs are steamed, but on the Gulf Coast they are boiled.

Italian food

Dishes from Italy are more popular than any other kind of 'foreign' food in the USA. Today, pizza is almost as American as it is Italian and some kinds of Italian foods are more popular in the USA than they are in Italy. In fact, Americans eat 18 acres of pizza every day! Not each of course.

This is partly because so many Italians came to live in the USA around 100 years ago – mostly between 1880 and 1920. These people started up 'Little Italys' – areas of Italian restaurants and food shops – and they used American produce – like meats, cheeses and flour – to create new dishes. They made the traditional American chophouse into the Italian steakhouse and the 'spaghetti house'.

When the Second World War ended, many American soldiers (or G.l.s) came back remembering the food they had eaten in Italy. When flights became cheaper, more Americans started to travel, and they wanted to eat the food they had experienced in Europe at home. Italian restaurants became more fashionable and sophisticated, serving expensive truffles, delicious wild mushrooms and wonderful wines.

Eating in space

American astronauts are famous all over the world. Because spaceships are small, there aren't any real kitchens, and as there is no gravity in space, special food needs to be taken on voyages.

Food in space needs to be in small pieces (because there is no gravity, food can really easily fly out of your mouth!). Drinks have to be half-solid for the same reason and must be drunk out of things a bit like toothpaste tubes. Food has to be freeze-dried so that it doesn't go bad during the long time it is in space.

Things have been improved so that food pieces are covered with a kind of jelly to stop them crumbling and making a mess in the spaceship. Dried food is injected with water through a kind of gun so it is softer – a bit like baby food – and can be fed through a tube into the astronaut's mouth.

Because there is no gravity in space, knives, forks and spoons are held with magnets to food trays to stop them flying off – although this sometimes happens anyway! The trays are then attached to the astronauts' legs with Velcro.

Hot, hot, hot

You may be surprised to find out that the chilli con carne is an American invention – not a Mexican one. Most experts think that it was first eaten in Texas around 150 years ago, when the cooks who fed the hungry cowboys on long journeys had to use whatever food they could find on the way. They found chilli and garlic growing wild, and used buffaloes and even rattlesnakes for meat! The dish soon became very popular – some people say that the great bank robbers Frank and Jesse James wouldn't rob a bank in a town which had their favourite chilli con carne restaurant. Then chilli became fashionable, so that when the actress Elizabeth Taylor was filming *Cleopatra* in Italy in the 1960s, she demanded that a famous American restaurant send her over her favourite dish.

Soul food

Soul food is African-American food in America. A lot of foods that are now common in the US originally came from Africa – including watermelons, pumpkins, okra, eggplant (called aubergine in Britain), cucumbers, onions and garlic. These foods came over when African slaves started to be brought over to North America in the early 1600s.

These slaves usually ate better foods than their owners. Slaves had to be strong to work so hard, so they ate lots of vegetables and drank no alcohol. The white Americans would eat lots of sweet and fatty foods, and drink spirits. Nothing was ever wasted in the slaves' cooking, so that leftovers were used to make croquettes or fritters and stale bread became bread pudding.

Today, what was once slave food is very popular in the USA and many other countries around the world. Soul food means dishes such as ribs, fried chicken, stewed okra and corn bread. Because of the large number of French people in Louisiana, dishes there often have creamy sauces.

Hamburgers

Hamburgers or beefburgers are probably the most popular food to come from the United States. They were probably invented more than 100 years ago, but it was several years later that they were first put into bread by a 15-year-old American boy called Charles Nagreen. He put some fried beef between slices of bread and sold it, calling it a hamburger.

One of the reasons why hamburgers became so popular was because they were so easy to eat 'on the road' – they were 'fast food'. The McDonald's chain began in the 1950s, and many other companies copied the idea.

Today, the average American eats three hamburgers each week! That's a total of about 38 billion in a year.

☞ **Ramps** are a kind of onion found in Appalachia. They are eaten as part of traditional ceremonies by native Americans but because they leave such a strong flavour on your breath some children eat them so they can be sent home from school!

☞ **Spam** "SPiced hAM" is tinned meat which was eaten by American soldiers in the Second World War. It is Hawaii's state food.

☞ **Stinkheads** sounds disgusting but it is a fish dish eaten by the Yup'ik Eskimos in Alaska which they think is delicious! They cut the heads off fish, usually salmon, and put them in the ground for the summer before digging them up.

☞ **Mountain oysters** are the testicles of young bulls which are eaten by cattle ranchers in the West and South of the US. They are normally rolled in batter and deep-fried. Hmmm.

☞ **Shoo-fly pie** – like the sound of this? It is a very sweet pie made with molasses (a thick, dark mixture of sugar). It gets its name because it has an open top and flies come to eat the molasses so they have to be shooed away!

As American as apple pie

In America there is a saying that when something is really American it is 'as American as apple pie'. But apple pie isn't American at all. Apple pies were probably first made by the ancient Greeks and then became popular in England in the 1500s. It was the English who then brought apple pies to the USA.

By 1878, they had become so popular that the famous American writer Mark Twain made a list of all the American food he missed while in Europe, which included 'Apple pie,

Peach pie, American mince pie, Pumpkin pie and Squash pie'.

How the crisp was invented

The crisp (or potato chip, as it known in the US) was invented in 1853 by someone called George Crum. George was a chef in a cafe in New York, USA. One day someone complained that the chips (or French fries, in American English) were too thick. Although George tried to make them thinner, the customer was still not happy. George then got annoyed and made some crisps that were so thin that it was impossible to eat them with a fork, hoping that it would make the customer angry. But he liked them and the crisp, or potato chip, has gone on to make lots of people very happy since.

Drinks

America is sometimes referred to as the land of plenty and whenever you are in restaurants or diners (like all-day cafés with a distinctive American feel), you will notice the size of portions and the enormous range of drinks and dishes. Often iced water is brought to the table of a restaurant, and fruit juices, milkshakes, coffee and iced tea are all really popular.

A Little Bit of Sport

The America's Cup

This sailing race gets its name from the big (25 inch) solid silver cup, (sometimes called 'the 'auld mug', that is presented to the winning yachtsmen). It was first won by the crew of the yacht *America*, representing the New York Yacht Club, which was on a visit to England in 1851, for the first Great Universal Exhibition. It was mostly just British and American sailors in the race, and the Americans won every year for 132 years! Then, in 1983, an Australian team won, which meant that the next race was held 'Down Under' in Australia. From then on it became an important international sports event. It is still one of the most difficult sailing challenges in the world.

Baseball

Baseball came to the United States before the American Civil War (1861–5) as the simple game of rounders. It became really popular in the 1920s, when 'Babe' Ruth (1895–1948) led the New York Yankees to several victories in the main baseball tournament, the World Series, and became a national hero. Over the decades, every team has had its great players. One of the most famous was the Brooklyn Dodgers' Jackie Robinson (1919–72), a brilliant athlete who became the first African-American player in the major leagues in 1947.

In the 1996 Olympics, it was a sign of baseball's appeal outside the United States that the contest for the gold medal came down to Japan and Cuba (Cuba won). Perhaps one day the World Series will be the international event that they thought it would be when they named it!

Curling

Curling is played with stones that are slid along ice with special brooms towards the 'goal'. It is one of the oldest sports in the world. People were playing it as long ago as the 1500s. No one knows exactly who invented it, but it was probably someone in Scotland. It was brought to the United States by Scottish soldiers during the French and Indian War in the 1700s.

Football

American football is a completely different game from the one played in Britain. It is just as popular, though. Crowds of 50,000 to 100,000 are normal at professional games, and millions more people watch them on TV. Football is basically an autumn sport, with teams playing from eight to 16 games, usually on successive weekends. The professional teams of the National Football League (NFL) end the season with the massive Super Bowl game, which usually gets one of the biggest TV audiences each year.

Basketball

Modern basketball came to the United States a little more than a 100 years ago, in 1891. A teacher was looking for a way for his naughty pupils to exercise indoors, as it was too cold to play outside. He remembered playing 'duck on a rock,' a game in which you had to try to knock a large rock off a boulder by throwing smaller rocks at it. So he nailed peach baskets at each end of a gym and challenged his students to throw a soccer ball into them from below.

Today as many as 200 million people a year go to basketball games in the US, which means that it is more popular than any other sport. In every state both boys and girls play basketball at school.

Ice hockey

Until just 20 years ago most people thought that ice hockey had come from English hockey (which is called 'field hockey' in North America), and had been spread throughout Canada by British soldiers in the mid-1800s. But then it was found that around 200 years ago the natives in the Canadian province of Nova Scotia played a very similar game. However it started, ice hockey quickly spread from Canada to the US, and the game is now dominated by US teams (including some that used to be based in Canada).

Skateboarding

The very first kind of skateboards – around 100 years ago – were actually more like scooters, with roller-skate wheels attached to a milk crate. Then, around 50 years ago, surfers in California wanted to come up with a way of surfing when the weather was bad. They began hammering roller-skate wheels on to planks of wood and went 'sidewalk surfing' along the streets. Children saw that this was a great city sport and people began to 'curb-jump' (or, as we'd write it in Britain, 'kerb-jump'). The 'Ollie,' invented by Alan Ollie Gelfand, is a jump into the air with the skateboard staying right under the feet. Today, skateboarding is the sixth most popular participant sport in the United States.

Softball

Softball is a kind of baseball. It was first played in Chicago on Thanksgiving Day, 1887. A group of young men were listening to the results of an important football game in a gym. One of them happened to pick up a boxing glove and threw it at someone. Of course the rules have changed since then!

Surfing

When the British explorer Captain James Cook landed in the islands of Hawaii, way back in 1778, he was surprised to find the men and women there – including members of the royal family – surfing. One of the oldest known surfboards in the world is thought to have belonged to Princess Kaneamona, who lived in the first half of the 1600s. Another expert surfer princess in Hawaii was Princess Kalulaini, who lived around 100 years ago. Surfing only really took off in the rest of the world around 50 years ago, beginning in towns along the coast of southern California on the southwest coast of the USA.

Volleyball

The sport of volleyball, originally called 'mintonette', was invented in 1895 by William G. Morgan, following the invention of basketball by only four years. Morgan, a graduate of the Springfield College of the YMCA, styled the game to be a blend of basketball, baseball, tennis and handball. Some people say that volleyball, like ice hockey, is similar to a game played by Native Americans, but it's not known if Morgan knew that when he invented volleyball.

Windsurfing and kiteboarding

Windsurfing is a cross between sailing and surfing, invented – not surprisingly – by a sailor and a surfer. This happened in southern California in the late 1960s. Windsurfing is now popular all over the world and became an Olympic sport in 1984.

Kiteboarding has only been around for 20 years or so. It's like windsurfing, but you are pulled along by large kites. This means that the people who do it can try daring tricks with scary names such as 'heart-attack' and 'boneless'.

Festivals
and
Celebrations

New Year's football parties

On New Year's Day the popular sport of American football is televised all day long and special parties are thrown. Food and drink at these parties may include submarine sandwiches, which are up to five feet long; potato chips, potato salad, pizza, pretzels, nuts and candy, and beer or soda pop (fizzy drinks).

The Rose Parade in Pasadena, California, is shown as part of the football broadcast. It was started in 1890 to resemble the Festival of Flowers in Nice, in southern France, and nowadays it uses more than 40,000 flowers.

Martin Luther King Day

The Rev. Martin Luther King, Junior, an African-American clergyman, is considered a great American because of his tireless efforts to win civil rights for all people through non-violent means. Since his assassination in 1968, memorial services have marked his birthday on 15 January. In 1986 the third Monday of January was declared a national holiday to honour King's memory.

Presidents' Day

Until the mid-1970s, 22 February was a national holiday, marking the birthday of George Washington, hero of the Revolutionary War and first President of the United States.

In addition, 12 February was a holiday in most states, marking the birthday of Abraham Lincoln, who was President during the Civil War. The two days have been joined and the holiday has been expanded to embrace all past presidents. It is celebrated on the third Monday in February.

A wonderful parade

In big cities in the US on Easter Sunday there are large parades in the street where people show off their new clothes and Easter bonnets. Often, the parade is led by someone carrying a candle or a cross.

Memorial Day

Celebrated on the fourth Monday of May, this holiday honours those soldiers who have died in combat. Although it originated after the American Civil War, it has become a day on which soldiers from all wars are remembered at special events held in cemeteries, churches and other public meeting places.

Happy birthday!

The Fourth of July, or Independence Day, celebrates America's 'birthday'. Well, really it celebrates the day that the 13 colonies *said* that they were independent from Great Britain: 4 July 1776, when the Declaration of Independence was signed. In fact the colonies did not really become independent until the end of the Revolutionary War, in 1783, and the United States did not exist until its constitution was written in 1787 – but none of that would have happened if the Declaration hadn't come first.

Americans have picnics, parades, concerts and fireworks on this day. Many people also fly the US flag. You might think that it became a holiday immediately after the signing of the Declaration of Independence, but actually it didn't become a tradition until after the War of 1812.

Labor Day

This holiday, on the first Monday in September, honours the nation's working people, typically with parades. For most Americans it marks the end of the summer vacation (which is what Americans call holidays) and, for many students, the beginning of the school year.

Columbus Day

On 12 October 1492 the Italian navigator Christopher Columbus landed in the New World. Although most other nations in the Americas observe this holiday on 12 October, in the United States it is marked on the second Monday in October.

Halloween

People in the United States celebrate Halloween much more than in Britain. But not many people know that many Halloween customs actually come from Ireland. Summer officially ended on 31 October and it was thought that on this day the spirits of anyone who had died in that year would come back, looking for living bodies to take over. So they had to do something to scare off the dead spirits and to do this they dressed up in scary costumes. In the 1840s Irish people escaping the country's potato famine brought their Halloween traditions with them to the United States. They used to make lanterns out of turnips, which were very common in Ireland, but later they discovered pumpkins were much easier to get hold of in their new homeland, so they used those instead.

Thank you!

Thanksgiving is celebrated only in the United States. The very first thanksgiving was held by the pilgrims from England in 1621 to say thank you to God for their first harvest in the country. Because of a very bad winter about half of them had died, so they had to ask for help from the nearby Native Americans, who taught them how to plant crops. It is very likely that the Native Americans were invited, and that everyone ate turkey and pumpkin, which is still eaten today.

Nowadays Thanksgiving Day is the fourth Thursday in November, but many American people take a day's holiday on the following Friday as well, so that they can have a four-day weekend.

Kwanzaa

Kwanzaa is one of America's newest holidays, but it is also one of its fastest-growing celebrations. It was started in 1966 by Maulana Karenga, a professor at California State University who thought that African-American people should celebrate their roots. The festival lasts from 26 December to 1 January. Its name means 'first fruits' – as in the first fruits of the harvest – and it is based on African harvest festivals. People light candles and sing, and think about one of seven main things on each of the seven days of the festival: unity, self-determination, collective work, co-operation, purposefulness, creativity and faith. On the first day one black candle is lit; then they light three red candles and then three green candles, one by one.

State fairs

Each state holds its own annual fair, with local themes and music. For many years these state fairs were mainly celebrations of farming. The very first fairs were started in the days when most people lived on farms, as a way of making farm life a bit more fun and having a party. Today only 2 per cent of Americans are involved in farming, so most state fairs celebrate industry too.

Ever since the 13 colonies formed the United States, other parts of the continent have had to apply for permission to become a state, from the 1790s right up to 1959, when Hawaii joined. To do this, they had to give the name of the state capital, create a state university and build state fairgrounds. Today some states use their fairs as a way to celebrate the day on which they joined the Union.

Festivals in the Northeast

The Fall Foliage Festival in Warner, New Hampshire, includes a wood-chopping contest and an auction to celebrate the autumn leaves turning spectacular shades of red, orange and yellow. People from all over the country and all over the world come to see the special sight.

In the part of Pennsylvania where the 'Pennsylvania Dutch' people live, locals celebrate their European heritage with seasonal festivals and parades. (In fact their roots are in Germany: 'Dutch' doesn't mean they came from the Netherlands, it's just the local way of saying Deutsch, which is the German word for 'German'.)

Fat Tuesday

Mardi Gras is a carnival that takes place every year in New Orleans. The name means 'Fat Tuesday' (in French), because in years gone by it was the last day for Catholics to eat what they wanted before they fasted for Lent. In many places around the world people eat pancakes on this day, in order to use up all the sugar, eggs and milk in their cupboards.

In New Orleans there is a big party with jazz bands, people in costumes and decorated floats. This first began when French people came to live here in the early 1700s. People throw

millions of coloured bead necklaces, cups and coins from the floats, which are moving cars or large displays decorated with fresh flowers or crepe paper by local groups and schools. The people who catch them believe they will have good luck. Musical groups march and play their instruments, and military bands also often take part.

Festivals in the Midwest

Winters are long in many Midwestern states, so winter festivals have become social events. In St Paul, Minnesota, the Winter Carnival offers exhibitions of skating, skiing and ice-fishing, and even snowmobile races. In Houghton Lake, Michigan, a winter festival called Tip-Up-Town USA offers a contest for the best sculpture carved in ice!

In St Maries, Idaho, during the Paul Bunyan Days in August, townspeople celebrate the legend of this giant American lumberjack by holding tree-cutting contests.

Every May the townspeople of Orange City, Iowa, and Holland, Michigan, celebrate their Dutch ancestry with Tulip Festivals (in these towns 'Dutch' does mean that their families came from the Netherlands!). Believe it or not, in southwest Oklahoma there is a festival of rattlesnakes. More than 40,000 people visit it every year in April. Lots of rattlesnakes live in this part of the USA, so here you can eat some rattlesnake meat, buy some things made out of rattlesnake or even ask rattlesnake hunters what makes rattlesnakes tick... or is it rattle...? Although it sounds like a crazy idea, the festival began quite sensibly in 1966, when it was decided that too many rattlesnakes were destroying local farmland.

Cowboys, Indians and musicians

In winter Aspen, Colorado, is a popular ski resort, but in the summer the town holds a music festival, where concerts and classes are offered in both classical and contemporary music. Many other holidays in the Southwest have a 'Wild West' theme. Tombstone, Arizona, celebrates Helidorado Days in the autumn, while in Tucson, also in Arizona, cowboys and Indians show their skills in La Festival de los Vaqueros (which is Spanish for 'the festival of the cowboys'). Lincoln, New Mexico, holds a fiddlers' convention, as well as Pony Express races in honour of the first US mail system, as part of its Lincoln County Days.

Festivals on the West Coast

Every year in Santa Barbara, California, there is a festival called 'Old Spanish Days' in the first week of August. It celebrates the many Hispanic people who live in the town with parades and dances. Kids throw 'confetti eggs' (eggs filled with confetti) at each other.

The northwestern state of Oregon boasts a rose festival in Portland, where bands play music in a parade of flowers and floats. In nearby Washington State spring is welcomed in with a Daffodil Festival offering a parade of floats made from these brilliant yellow flowers.

Celebrating the midnight sun

The town of Kodiak has a King Crab Festival during the crab-harvesting season in May, but in most parts of the state the serious festival season is in June. Like Scandinavia, Alaska is so far north that in summer you can see the 'midnight sun'. During the weekend closest to the summer solstice on 21 June people celebrate 22 hours of direct sunlight each day with a parade, street dances, barbeques and softball games. The city of Nome has daylight for almost 24 hours a day in June, so raft races and midnight baseball games are the main events at its Midnight Sun Festival.

Flowers all year round

Hawaii is warm the whole year round, and flower festivals were held there even before it became a state. Garlands of flowers, called *leis*, are given to people on almost any special occasion, including birthdays, anniversaries and farewell parties. If you are celebrating a special occasion you may get so many garlands around your neck that they start to cover your face!

The very first garlands were made way back when people first came to live on the islands and gave *leis* to their gods during religious ceremonies. Then farmers put them around their own necks to receive blessings for their crops and pregnant women wore them to give them the power of life.

These days 1 May is known as Lei Day. This festival was set up by a poet, author and artist called Don Blanding, who fell in love with the Hawaiian islands.

Emergency Phrases

Although people in the United States speak English, there are many words that are different from British ones. When Americans says pants they actually mean trousers. Underpants is what they would say for pants. 'Sneakers' mean 'trainers' to an American. They say 'sidewalk' for pavement, 'apartment' for flat and 'movie' for film. And 'gas' in the US is wasn't what you might think. It's petrol!

Also, people in different parts of the country don't always speak in the same way – they have their own accents and vocabulary. Americans tend to speak more slowly and clearly than British people. In fact, some Americans say that it seems like British folk 'swallow' their words.

How do you spell that?

It can be confusing because even when Americans use the same words as English ones, they often spell them differently. For example:

☞ British people spell: cen**tre**, but the American version is: cen**ter**

☞ Thea**tre** is the UK spelling, but thea**ter** is American

☞ The UK version spells real**ise** like this. In the USA it's real**ize**

☞ It you were talking about something on TV in Britain, it would be a progr**amme**; in the USA it would be a progr**am**

☞ The British spell travelled with two 'l's'; for Americans it is traveled

☞ A neighbour is UK spelling. A neighbor is American

☞ Then there's the colour grey in the UK spelling. But in the USA it would be the color (with no 'u') gray.

British and American words

Some words used only in the USA actually came from Britain, but we stopped using them. For example:

☞ Fall (for autumn)

☞ Deck (as in a pack of cards)

☞ Noon (instead of midday)

☞ Molasses (instead of treacle)

☞ Back and forth (instead of backwards and forwards),

☞ Trash (for rubbish)

Americans have a reputation for loving money and they have a lot of different slang words connected with it. There's 'dough' and 'small change,' which both mean cash. Then there's 'not worth a red cent,' for something that's worthless and 'flat broke,' and 'dead broke,' for those with no money who can always 'bet their bottom dollar'.

The phrase 'to keep a stiff upper lip' might sound very British, but it was actually invented in 19th-century America. And lots of phrases said in Britain actually came from the USA. Like:

☞ 'fly off the handle' (when you get angry)

☞ 'sit on the fence' (when you don't take sides)

☞ 'bark up the wrong tree' (when you get the wrong idea)

☞ 'pull the wool over one's eyes' (trick someone)

☞ 'get hitched' (get married)

☞ 'face the music' (look at the problem)

☞ 'keep your shirt on' (don't get cross)

But the most important expression America has given to Britain and the rest of the world is 'OK' . Even in countries where they can't say it, they form a circle with their thumb and first finger and put their other fingers in the air instead. It seems it was first printed in 1839 as a short version of 'Oll Korrect'.

That's slang, man

Young people in Britain and the rest of the world use some American words to sound cool. Do you ever say: *Cool, wicked, chill,* or *nerd?* These all come from the USA.

Pidgin

Pidgin is another kind of slang. In Hawaii, pidgin is a combination of English, Hawaiian, Japanese, Filipino, Chinese and Portuguese. It is spoken on the streets and is certainly not a language that is taught in schools! Many words are a short or lazy version of an English word or expression.

☞ **An den**: What happened next.

☞ **Brah/bruddah**: Like 'brother' or 'mate', as in 'Eh, brah!'

☞ **Fo' what?**: Why? How come? (as in 'For what?')

☞ **Fo' real?**: Are you sure? (as in 'For real?')

☞ **Garans**: guaranteed (meaning: definitely)

☞ **Haaah?**: Sorry, I didn't hear you.

☞ **Howzit**: How are you?

☞ **Kay den**: OK then.

☞ **Whaddsdascoops**: What's going on?

People in different states say things differently. In Texas in the south, people often use Spanish words (because they are close to Mexico where they speak Spanish). They might say

'*Hola*,' for hello, or '*Qué pasa*?' instead of '*what's happening*?' '*Adiós*' for 'goodbye' and '*amigo*' instead of friend.

Texans also speak with an accent, which is known as a 'drawl' because they draw out words. Some words you might hear in Texas are:

- ☞ **All the fixins** – this is all the extras you might have with your big steak – like beans, mashed potatoes, gravy.

- ☞ **Awl** – 'Oil', which is Texas's largest industry.

- ☞ **Big ol'** – Large.

- ☞ **Buffalo chip** – cow dung.

- ☞ **Dadgummit** – like 'damn'.

- ☞ **Fixin' to** – meaning to. As in 'I'm fixin' to get myself a piece of chicken'.

- ☞ **Gimme cap** – Baseball caps that are given out free because they advertise oil and other companies.

- ☞ **Give me a holler** – Call or write to me.

- ☞ **Howdy, y'all** – You might think that only cowboys in films say this for 'hello', but they still say it in Texas.

- ☞ **I reckon** – I think.

- ☞ **Over yonder** – Over there.

- ☞ **Yankee** – British people might sometimes call Americans 'Yankees', but Texans use it to mean someone from the north – that is anyone from outside of Texas.

- ☞ **Yes ma'am** – A polite way to answer a woman.

- ☞ **Yessir** and **nossir** – as in 'Yes sir' and 'no sir'.

Cowboys

The country's cowboys have a language all their own. They call a wild horse a bronco and when they are hungry they want 'chuck' which means food. When a cowboy goes to a dance, it's a 'shindig' and if someone disagrees with him he says he 'sold his saddle'.

Good Books

Non-fiction

AAA Adventures Across the USA: A Kid's Road Atlas

Bennett, William J., *The Children's Book of America*, Simon and Schuster

Furbee Mary Rodd, *Outrageous Women of Colonial America*, Wiley

Kalogiera, Dino, *Children's Map of the USA*, Konemann

King, David C., *Pioneer Days*, Wiley

Patrick, Diane, *Amazing African American History: A Book of Answers for Kids*, Wiley

Presidents of the USA, Autumn Publishing

Sutcliffe, Andrea, *Amazing US Geography: A Book of Answers for Kids*, The New York Library

Fiction

Little Lord Fauntleroy by Frances Hodgson Burnett, Dover Evergreen Classics
A tale about an American boy who is taken from the streets of nineteenth-century New York to his grandfather's English manor.

The Prince and the Pauper by Mark Twain, Penguin Classics.
A classic about a beggar and a prince who swap places.

America Street: A Multicultural Anthology of Stories Mazer, Moose Street
Tells of multi-ethnic experiences with 14 stories about teenagers whose parents or grandparents immigrated to the U.S.

My Heart is on the Ground: *The Diary of Nannie Little Rose, a Sioux Girl*, Dear America Series, Scholastic Inc.
A story of a small girl stuck between two cultures.

Wicked Websites

www.50states.com
Lots of information about the states and their capitals

www.americaslibrary.gov
Short stories and photographs about 'America's story'

www.americatakingaction.com
A national network of school websites

www.enchantedlearning.com
An excellent searchable site with short printable books, and special features such as 'President's Day' and 'Black History Month'

www.jefferson.lib.co.us/kids
Lots of facts on everything from American cooking to the US government

www.kids.gov
A US government site with subjects such as arts and computers as well as games and activities

www.kidsnewsroom.org
News from the USA and around the world, written for children

www.library.thinkquest.org search engine: enter 'USA' in 'Search'.
Detailed information on history, sport, science, etc., with lots of links

www.whitehouse.gov/kids/
Fun, with lots of facts. Just for children.

Quirks and Scribbles